SPOONER

A BIOGRAPHY

William Hayter

W. H. ALLEN · London
A Howard & Wyndham Company
1977

**This book is to be returned on or before
the last date stamped below.**

RENEWALS *Please quote:*
date of return, your ticket number
and computer label number for
each item.

SPOONER

A BIOGRAPHY

W. A. Spooner in 1913.
From the portrait in New
College Hall by Hugh
Rivière.

To Esme
who may come
to New College
one day

Contents

List of Illustrations

Note on Illustrations

The Frontispiece and Plates III-VII are reproductions of pictures belonging to the Warden and Fellows of New College, and are reproduced with their permission.

Plate I is a reproduction of a portrait in the National Portrait Gallery, London.

Plate II is from the archives of the Junior Common Room of New College. I am grateful to Mr Miles Young, former Steward of the Junior Common Room, for drawing my attention to it.

Plates VIII and IX are from photograph albums in the possession of Mrs Arthur Murray, Spooner's daughter. I am grateful to her daughter, Mrs I. M. Crombie, for having made them available to me. Unfortunately there are no dates in these albums.

Like everyone who illustrates a book on an Oxford subject, I am deeply indebted to Mr J. W. Thomas, of Thomas Photos, for invaluable help. All the illustrations except Plate I are based on reproductions made by him.

Introduction

THERE ARE NOT many individuals in our history whose surnames have given a word to the English language, without a capital letter. Sandwich, mackintosh, wellingtons, cardigan, boycott, lynch, bowdlerise; there must be a few more. W. A. Spooner, Warden of New College, Oxford from 1903 to 1924, became by perhaps unmerited accident a member of this little band. There are those who maintain that he never uttered a spoonerism, but there the word stands, his chief monument. It is conceivable that he deserves no other. His own description of himself, typically modest and also typically acute, is 'a moderately useful man'. This is not far from the mark. But he was, for more than sixty uninterrupted years, a member of one of the oldest and largest of the Oxford colleges, and these years happened to be particularly interesting ones in the history of the College, and indeed of the University. They were the years in which Oxford was forced out of its centennial sloth and became a modern university. New College, Spooner's college, was as the period began one of the most slothful of them all. Before his arrival, entry to it was confined to former scholars of Winchester College. Spooner himself was the first non-Wykehamist to be elected a

Scholar of New College, the first non-Wykehamist to be elected a Fellow, and the first non-Wykehamist to be elected Warden since the college's foundation in the late fourteenth century. Spooner found New College a small, closed society, an anomaly and almost a scandal; when he retired it had become one of the leading colleges in the University.

It seemed therefore that a life of Spooner, while illuminating an entertaining, peculiar and in many ways attractive personality, might also throw some light on an important period in one of the country's major educational establishments. There are various sources for such a life. New College has a rich fund of oral tradition about Spooner. This is of course quite untrustworthy. Fortunately the College has recently come into possession of some much more reliable material. Spooner's daughter Rosemary, who died in 1976, deposited with New College some chapters of her father's incomplete and unpublished autobiography, two volumes of an intermittently kept diary and a number of interesting letters. The college archives already contained his notes on College meetings during his Wardenship and on his progresses round the College estates. Finally there are still many people alive who remember him. I myself, as an undergraduate at New College in the twenties, lunched with him in his North Oxford home after his retirement. I retain from this occasion nothing more than a vivid impression of his 'shrimp-like figure' (the phrase is Sir Roy Harrod's), but fortunately other old members of the College have more lively and interesting recollections of their encounters with 'the Spoo', the name by which most of them seem to refer to him.

Valuable though they are, these sources are not without

their defects. The oral traditions are, as has been said, un-reliable. The personal recollections, of course, only apply to Spooner's later years. His own material is full of gaps. The autobiography, entitled *Fifty Years in an Oxford College*, can be dated by that title as having been written in 1912, since he was elected a Scholar of New College in 1862, though in the opening words of the typescript – 'It is fifty years and a little more since I came to Oxford' – he has inserted the manuscript word 'one' after 'fifty'. In a letter to his wife written on board ship on 7 April 1912, on his way to South Africa, he writes 'I have done some remini-scences, but they seem to me too trivial to be quite worth recording'. There are various confusing drafts and re-drafts, and many omissions. He says nothing in the autobiography, for instance, about his parents or his background, and does not even tell us where and when he was born. Indeed, after the first few paragraphs he says very little about himself, and the ensuing chapters become in the main general reflections about Oxford life and Oxford personalities. His own life is not recorded beyond the early days of his Fellowship, when the autobiography breaks off; according to Rosemary Spooner he gave it up because he felt that his memory was not vivid enough. He began writing his diary in 1881, when he was thirty-seven. The first volume ends in 1883. The second volume, dated February 1890, begins 'I have six weeks of diary to write up, for it is the ninth of February to-day and I wish to keep the record of the year. I have dropped my diary for a good while as I had tired of it'. This leaves it uncertain whether there were any intervening volumes; if there were they have disappeared. He then keeps going, with diminishing detail, until 1897. Then there is a gap of six years until, in 1903, he records the beginning of his time as Warden. The diary then continues, more or less, until September 1907. Then there is a gap until 1924, when he describes his resignation; the last entries record the installation of his successor, H. A. L. Fisher, in January 1925.

Neither the autobiography nor the diaries seem publishable in their entirety. The autobiography contains long parentheses, many of them accounts of the personalities and achievements of individuals whose fame has not endured. The diaries are full of domestic details of a trivial kind. But both also include a wealth of interesting material, and very extensive quotations from them will be found in this book. Indeed I have tried as far as possible to tell his story in his own words; this book is at least as much a self-portrait as a portrait.

The autobiography consists of:
A. Four type-written chapters, entitled
   I   School and Undergraduate Days
   II   The Tutorial Staff and what I owed to Them
   III The University in my Undergraduate Days
   IV   Religious, Intellectual and Social Life in the Early
        Days of my Fellowship 1867–1877 (much re-written
        and parts scored through).

B. Two quarto notebooks with manuscript drafts.
   1. The first notebook begins with a chapter heading, Chapter 5 (scored through and replaced by 4) The Charity Organisation Society, the Board of Guardians, the Oxford Political Economy Club. Most of this is scored through and unrevised, and the manuscript then continues with the subjectof A. IV above. This occurs in several versions, often scored through, and

yet another version is on some loose sheets inserted at the end.

2. The second notebook, which begins rather bafflingly with the words 'On the other hand' but does not seem to be in sequence with any of the earlier drafts, is at first yet another continuation, or revised version, of A.IV. Then comes a section headed 'Reform in College and in the University 1870–1877', which covers much of the same ground. Next is a section headed 'Chapter 7. The Commission of 1877 and its results'. This seems to have been written originally on left-hand pages only; another version was subsequently written on the right-hand pages. Next comes a section headed 'The University and the Colleges in the Eighties'; here again two alternative versions appear on left-hand and right-hand pages. Finally there is one short section on a loose sheet headed 'Chapter VIII. The growth of the Married Fellow and Tutor system in Oxford'.

There is also a loose sheet indicating what Spooner meant to do next. Chapter IX was to have been about Building in Oxford, Jowett's Vice-Chancellorship, the Indian Institute and Indian Studies and Reform of the Commemoration. Chapter X was to cover the death of Jowett and of Alfred Robinson and 'the Rise of the Young Spirit'. These chapters seem not to have been even drafted.

In addition to those mentioned above the College archives contain two other major Spooner items; these are: 1. A series of letters to Mrs Spooner written during his tour of South Africa in 1912. These are not in their original manuscript, but typed out to form a continuous record after his return.

2. A paper headed *Two Oxford Reformers, Mark Pattison and Benjamin Jowett*. This is evidently the paper mentioned in his diary as having been read to the New College Essay Society in January 1925, after his retirement.

It will be evident from the above that no life of Warden Spooner could have been attempted without the material which Rosemary Spooner deposited with the college. But I am indebted to her not only for this material but for patiently answering a whole series of probably tiresome questions about her father and her family, and for having in fact completed a long written questionnaire on the subject. Unfortunately her death in February 1976 made it impossible to show her the book in its completed form.

I must also record my particular indebtedness to two other individuals. Mr Francis Steer, the College archivist, assembled all the Spooner material from the archives for me, and kindly handed over to me his own collection of Spooneriana. He also effectively followed up a number of enquiries that I put to him. Some years ago Mr Reginald Jennings of Marlborough College, an old member of New College, started to collect material for a life of Spooner. The result seemed inadequate for the task (this was before Rosemary Spooner's material became available) and he put it aside, but when he heard of my intentions he kindly handed over to me all the documents he had collected, many of which are incorporated in this book.

I am grateful to Mrs C. D. Shane and the Authorities of the Lick Observatory Archives, University of California at Santa Cruz, for permission to reproduce the account of a visit to the Spooners which appears on page 112.

Next I must express my gratitude to those old members

of New College, and others, who have produced personal recollections of Spooner, and have called my attention to useful sources of information or have helped me to identify persons, places and incidents mentioned in the Spooner material, among others Mr Alexander Ando, Mr A. J. P. Andrews, Sir John Balfour, Mr Desmond Browne, Mrs Ethel Burney, Mr David Butler, Professor Morton Cohen, Sir Christopher Cox, Viscount Furneaux, Dr J. A. Gibson, Professor William C. Gibson, Dr J. B. Hainsworth, Sir Roy Harrod, Colonel Victor Hill, Professor E. M. Hugh-Jones, Sir Julian Huxley, Mr A. Maclehose, Sir Max Mallowan, Professor Charles Manning, Mr T. S. Matthews, Dr Nathaniel Micklem, Mr J. B. Murgatroyd, Dr Rosemary Murray, Mr Horner Parshall, Dr J. M. Potter, Professor H. H. Price, Mr D. W. Pye, Mr A. M. Quinton, Mr John Rolt, Mary Duchess of Roxburghe, Mr John Sparrow, Mr S. E. Thompson, Mr Christopher Turner, the Very Reverend Donald Selby Wright, and Mr Larzer Ziff. I am also very grateful for assistance from the staff of the Bodleian Library, from the Reference and Registry Section of the BBC, from the newspaper section of the British Museum Library at Colindale and above all from Mrs Feneley of New College Library. Finally I must put on record the debt I owe to my secretary, Mrs Joan Hawkins, who managed to decipher my own untidy manuscript and the much clearer hand of Warden Spooner and who in addition to typing out the whole book solved several difficult problems for me.

CHAPTER I

The Beginning

ALL HIS LIFE, Spooner looked like a white-haired baby. His appearance hardly changed. He was small, pink-faced and an albino, with a disproportionately large head and very short-sighted pale blue eyes.

This strange little creature was born on 22 July 1844, at 17 Chapel Street, off Grosvenor Place, in London, the eldest son of William Spooner, a county court judge for North Staffordshire. This William Spooner was the son of another William Spooner, who was Archdeacon of Coventry, and one of his sisters married Archibald Campbell Tait, later Archbishop of Canterbury and the father-in-law of Randall Davidson, another Archbishop of Canterbury. The Archdeacon of Coventry's sister, Barbara Spooner, married William Wilberforce, the Abolitionist, and was the mother of Samuel Wilberforce, Bishop successively of Oxford and Winchester. The Wilberforces seem not to have approved of Barbara and her family; one of them described her as 'the only religious member of a worldly family'. But this was a misjudgment, at least of the other Spooners. William Wilberforce described his brother-in-law, the Archdeacon of Coventry, as 'so truly a good man that it must be useful to anyone to be his associate', and another brother, Richard Spooner, came to the rescue when, in 1830, Wilberforce's eldest son got into financial difficulties. In fact the Spooners were, as Lord Furneaux, William Wilberforce's latest biographer, puts it, 'a respectable and thoroughly serious Evangelical family from Birmingham', and the little albino, also christened William (with the addition of Archibald after Archibald Tait who was his godfather) was born into the ecclesiastical purple. He himself never rose higher in the Church's hierarchy than an Honorary Canonry of Christ Church. But he was the grandson of one archdeacon and the brother of another, the cousin of one bishop and the son-in-law of another, and his aunt and one of his cousins were both married to Archbishops of Canterbury; a niece married W. R. Inge, the 'Gloomy Dean' of St Paul's.

A. C. Tait, the future archbishop who was Spooner's uncle by marriage and his godfather, was at the time of Spooner's birth Headmaster of Rugby, (in succession to Thomas Arnold), a dry, formidable, powerful figure of whom the *Dictionary of National Biography* observes that 'no archbishop probably since the Reformation has had so much weight in Parliament or in the country generally'. There was one surprising element in Tait's history. His sister married a Sitwell, and he himself was brought up at Renishaw and eventually became the guardian of Sir George Sitwell, the father of Edith, Osbert and Sacheverell. There is a certain incongruity between these flamboyant patricians and the dour Scottish prelate, and Tait must have felt more at home in the Spooners' Evangelist world. Sir Osbert Sitwell attributes his father's atheism largely to Tait's ultra-religious zeal. Tait's Spooner godson must have been more congenial to him, and Spooner's diary is full of testimony to Tait's powerful influence and to the affectionate respect in which he held his godfather.

Not much can be discovered about Spooner's childhood. In his diary, writing of a visit to an uncle's house near Leeds, he says 'the place brings back some of the few pleasant memories of my childhood', which does not suggest very happy early days. A slightly happier note is struck in a letter he wrote in 1919 to the then Dean of Carlisle, in which he refers to 'many associations with the Deanery, the earliest dating from more than sixty-five years ago, when I stayed with the Taits in the Deanery and I can remember watching the trains out of my nursery window'. In his autobiography he only tells us that 'I was brought up in Oswestry School in Shropshire near the borders of Wales, being sent there because my father was for the time resident in Wales'. Spooner's father is a somewhat mysterious figure. According to the *Dictionary of National Biography* he was a county court judge and lived at Walton Lodge, Stafford, but there are stories of him prospecting in Wales, and others of his wife in tears about his extravagance and unpaid bills. On the first page of his diary his son writes:

> My father died in May of last year, May 1880. He was a man of many remarkable gifts – warm, sympathetic, great quickness of perception, a good judge of character, just and upright. He had also an excellent memory and a good taste in poetry and art. His character was spoilt by a certain self-indulgence and by want of perseverance and self-control.

Of his mother Spooner writes (in the present tense as she was still alive)

She is subject to great fits of nervousness and depression, losing under their influence her powers of control, but, when she is well, she has a clear sound judgment and good sense, much deep though not quick feeling, great conscientiousness and desire to do right, expressing itself sometimes in a rather cold and formal way. She has been trained up to live life much by rule and lives it so.

Possibly Spooner's father's self-indulgence, and the unpaid bills, may explain why his son was sent not to a conventional public school but to the Grammar School at Oswestry. About this school he has some interesting comments in the first chapter of his autobiography.

Oswestry was, with the exception of Shrewsbury, the most famous school of the Welsh border and also the most ancient. It celebrated its five hundredth anniversary six years ago, only fifteen years after Winchester, the oldest of our Public Schools, had kept its quincentenary. Oswestry was, in many ways, a rather typical Grammar School of the older sort, and had the characteristic merits and defects of those institutions. It contained from sixty to eighty boys, two-thirds perhaps boarders, one-third day-boys. It gave them an education superior to the Elementary, superior also in my view, to the scientific education which the more modern type of Secondary School mainly supplies. The moral tone and gentlemanly feeling of the boys was not always good; at times they became, when evil influences prevailed, deplorably bad; but there was a healthy admixture of classes to be found in the school, and society was not then cut up, as far as education was concerned, into these horizontal layers, which the spread of the boarding Public School has done so much to bring about, and the compulsory provision of free places in Secondary Schools so little to mitigate. In the old Grammar Schools boys of different ranks mixed freely together; they came to know, to understand, and, where respect was possible to respect one another. A certain amount of neighbourliness and comradeship were in this way established between the different classes, which are almost impossible where the children of different social rank are brought up in entirely different schools.

It is interesting to find the Warden of New College, before the First World War, expressing views about the impact of the Public Schools on the class structure resembling so closely those accepted by Labour Party educational reformers in the second half of the century. He follows up these comments with some remarks, less likely to be acceptable in those quarters, on the respective merits of the Classics and of Mathematics and Natural Science as instruments of education. Needless to say he is a strong partisan of the former. The Classics, he believes, awaken mental activity and alertness in a way which no other discipline can rival, whereas the sciences

> appeal rather to the memory. . . . It need not surprise us if a boy, classically or linguistically educated, makes often, if he is a boy of ability, quite extraordinarily rapid progress in natural science when he comes to study it; and leaves the boy who has been from the outset scientifically trained, far behind. This, I think, is the experience of most schoolmasters and of most College Tutors.

(Spooner here irresistibly recalls the story of the wife of a former Warden of All Souls who was once overheard saying of her husband 'The Warden could get up science in a fortnight if he wanted to'.) As for mathematics, the study of it, 'so far from quickening a boy's interest in things and speculations going on in the world around him, seems often to withdraw it and deaden it, and so leaves him, except in the line of his own special study, somewhat listless and helpless'.

After this characteristic parenthesis Spooner reverts to Oswestry School. His first headmaster there evidently neglected his pupils, leaving them to 'subordinates, who were not always efficient, and in some cases were not men of high character'. But in 1858 he was succeeded by the Rev. W. F. Short, 'a man of great energy, of fine character and many gifts and accomplishments – a man of taste, a fair scholar, a keen climber and sportsman, a great oar, a good geologist'. Spooner tells us that this paragon lacked application, and so, though he did well at first for a time, in a great variety of lines, 'he tired of them all in a few years and quitted them a comparative failure'. Meanwhile, however, he clearly had a great impact on young Spooner's intellectual development, stimulating his interest in the Classics. Moreover in one particular respect he settled the course of his young pupil's whole life. 'Mr Short', Spooner tells us, 'was a Fellow of New College, and it was to this fact that I owe my introduction to New College'.

CHAPTER II

Scholar of New College

SPOONER WAS ADMITTED to New College, after failing to enter Corpus Christi College, in October 1862, at an interesting and indeed critical moment in the College's history. New College, architecturally one of the grandest and most beautiful of the Oxford colleges, was by the middle of the nineteenth century in a rather sad condition. At the time of its foundation, in the late fourteenth century, its founder, William of Wykeham, had laid down that entry to it was to be reserved for those educated at his other foundation, Winchester College. This was because he wished the members of his Oxford College to have a sound preliminary education and distrusted, no doubt with reason, the grammar school education provided elsewhere in his time. But the best intentions of educational founders often go astray, and in fact this tight connection between the two institutions did not work out to the advantage of either. In their early days the school and the College produced some distinguished servants of Church and State, as Wykeham had intended. But after a century or two a kind of rigid torpor set in. 'I have often wondered', wrote Archbishop Laud in 1635 to the Bishop of Winchester, Visitor of the two colleges, 'why so many good scholars come from

Winchester to New College, and yet so few of them afterwards prove eminent men'. And at about this time there
was an ugly saying that New College contained 'golden
Scholars, silver Bachelors, leaden Masters, wooden Doctors'.
Laud attributed this downhill progress to the baleful
influence of Calvin's Institutions, Antony Wood to 'their
rich Fellowships they have, especially to their ease and good
diet, in which they excel any College else'. Others, with
perhaps greater plausibility, explained the low level of New
College achievement by the exclusive Winchester connection. Boys from among the seventy scholars at Winchester, who had obtained their places there by a system of
nomination, got places at New College by rotation, and
immediately became Fellows, for two years on a nominal
probation and thereafter for life or until marriage. When
they married, a College living generally became available.
No effort was required of them. Members of the College,
by a further perversion of its founder's intentions, did not
apply for the degrees of the University but awarded themselves their own degrees. Macaulay was one of those who
thought that the Winchester connection was the explanation of the College's decline. In his essay on Lord Bacon he
observes that Archbishop Whitgift, when Master of
Trinity College, Cambridge, 'stood up manfully against
those who wished to make Trinity College a mere append-
age to Westminster School; and by this act, the only good
act, so far as we remember, of his long public life, he saved
the noblest place of education in England from the degrading fate of King's College and New College' (King's
College, Cambridge, was bound to Eton as New College
was to Winchester).

Whatever the cause, there is no doubt that New College,

by the early seventeenth century, had ceased to perform the functions for which Wykeham had designed it. It produced no distinguished men between the Middle Ages and the nineteenth century. Rashdall and Rait, the historians of the College, observe that between the death of Warden Pink, in 1647, and the accession of Warden Shuttleworth in 1822 no Warden of the College wrote a book. These Wardens were a dreary succession. Their heavy, dull portraits stare stupidly down from the walls of the Warden's Lodgings. One of them, John Oglander, got himself painted by Romney, and it was during his Wardenship that the College commissioned Sir Joshua Reynolds to produce designs for the glass-painting in the great west window of the Ante-Chapel. His memorial tablet was designed by Wyatt and executed by Westmacott. So he at least seems to have been a man of taste. There is no evidence that any of the others were. And many of them were even corrupt. The Wardenship of Winchester was in the gift of New College. The Founder had intended this to be an inferior position (for instance, the Warden of Winchester was only to keep two horses, to the Warden of New College's six). But the Warden of Winchester found he could screw much more money out of the Winchester endowments at the expense of the little boys entrusted to his charge than the Warden of New College could out of the powerful body over which he presided. So the Wardens of New College managed, in steady succession, to get themselves appointed Warden of Winchester, until the Visitor put a stop to it.

The clearest picture of New College in these deplorable days is to be found in the diaries of Parson Woodforde. Woodforde, describing his life in his New College living of Weston Longville in Norfolk, is delightful. But his account of his time at New College itself is depressing to read, a dreary catalogue of idleness, 'dull and deep potations' (as Gibbon describes the comparable contemporary scene at Magdalen) interspersed with pointless gambling, no study, no learning, no teaching, but also no apparent enjoyment of life. Antony Wood had described the College in 1682 as 'much given to drinking and gaming and vaine loutish pleasure'. It had clearly not altered in the eighteenth century. Sydney Smith, perhaps the most famous New College man before modern times, never alludes to the College in any of his writings, though he was a Fellow for eleven years; it is not surprising, he cannot have found it amusing.

Rashdall and Rait date the reform of the College from the Wardenship of John Shuttleworth (1822–1840). This is perhaps premature. Shuttleworth was quite an interesting man. His 'Ode to Learning', published in the *Gentleman's Magazine*, contains the well-known couplet

> Oh! make me Sphere-descended Queen
> A Bishop – or, at least, a Dean.

He became Bishop of Chichester in the end. And he invented the port railway, the ingenious mechanism that carries the decanters across in front of the fire in the Senior Common Room. He was a strong Evangelical, and his sudden and premature death, two years after his appointment to Chichester, was described by Dr Pusey as 'a token of God's presence in the Church of England'. But he was not exactly a reformer. True, he persuaded the College to renounce its out-of-date privilege of awarding its own degrees, largely no doubt because these degrees were by then seen to be worthless. But when, in his successor's time, the first

University Commission of 1850 (of which A. C. Tait, Spooner's godfather, was a member) was appointed, the College put up a stiff resistance to reform. It refused to divulge its Statutes to the Commissioners, and resisted all proposals for change. The Commission was subsequently given powers to issue ordinances, and finally did so in respect of New College in 1856. Under these the original seventy Fellowships of the College were to be replaced by thirty Fellowships and thirty Scholarships. Fifteen Fellowships were thrown open to competition, and the rest were reserved for members of Winchester or New College. All the Scholarships were, in the first instance, restricted to members of Winchester (who might, however, be Commoners of that school and not, as in the past, Scholars only, and Winchester had, at the same time, given up the system of nominations to its Scholarships and opened them to free competition); if no adequate Wykehamist were found for a Scholarship it was to be 'thrown open for that term to general competition'. The first Open Scholar elected under this clause was Spooner.

He describes his early days in the College in the first chapter of his autobiography, beginning with

two incidents connected with my election as Scholar which have impressed themselves on my memory. While I was walking round the College Quadrangle, between two of the papers, Ring, then the College Porter, himself a memorable figure, came up to me, and pointing out one of the Fellows whispered in my ear in a voice of mingled awe and disapprobation, 'That gentleman has just joined the Church of Rome, and ceases therefore to be a Fellow of the College'. The Porter was right; it was in those days a necessary consequence of joining the Church of Rome to be deprived of the enjoyment of a Fellowship. Later, after the repeal of the Test Act, this was no longer the case; and in two or three instances Fellows of Colleges continued to hold as Roman Catholics, Fellowships which they had won as members of the Church of England, and in later years Roman Catholics have with general approbation been elected to Fellowships. The other incident relates to myself. I was small, and very boyish in appearance when I first came up to Oxford and young in my ways for my years; one of my competitors for the scholarship was heard to remark – 'I do not mind who gets the scholarship, if that *child* does not'; but the *child* was elected. Four years of undergraduate life must have added to my age and the dignity of my appearance, for when at the end of my undergraduate time I was standing for a Fellowship at New College, the Senior Fellow of the College, coming in to inspect the candidates as we sat in Hall and noting my white hair, observed, 'Is he not rather old to be elected?' Another and later incident I also recall. While I was still an undergraduate, the Preacher in Chapel, using perhaps a sermon originally intended for a different congregation, addressed some of his hearers as those who had grown 'grey in sin'; my comrades insisted that I must have been the person designated, since I was the only member of the congregation to whom the designation could possibly apply.

He lived in College throughout his time as an undergraduate, first in rooms in the Front Quadrangle ('rather dark and cheerless') and then in the Garden Quadrangle where, on becoming a Fellow, he

took possession of what I think to be the most delightful rooms in College, those on the sunny side of the quadrangle overlooking the Garden. These, which I retained till my marriage, when I gave them up and took others less desirable, had been occupied not long before my time by Augustus Hare, whose life as Rector of Alton Barnes, Augustus Hare the younger describes in *Memorials of a Quiet Life*.

As an undergraduate he was, it seems, troubled by musical neighbours ('a Philistine I was born', he says elsewhere in the autobiography, 'and a Philistine in many respects I still remain').

The man in the room under me practised on the violin, but he knew only one tune and broke down in that always at the same point, which, having reached, he began it all over again. My neighbour on the other side kept an harmonium, and I remember his going right through Psalm CXIX on a chant played with one or two fingers.

The musical inflictions of present-day undergraduates would be very different in kind, though not perhaps in intensity.

Other sides of College life were still more different. In the slype outside the City Wall, where present-day Fellows park their cars, were stables, shanties built against the Wall, for the horses of those of the Fellows who kept them.

Many of the older generation of Fellows had been famous horsemen who had kept their horses in these inadequate stables. There still remained, when first I joined the College, the tradition of one of them who finally lost his life in a tandem accident, and used to spend his Sundays, when not engaged in Chapel or Hall, in flicking off the heads of the daisies in the Garden with his 'four in hand' whip. The number of Fellows who kept horses had diminished in my time, but, as Bursar, Mr L. J. Lee kept a couple of hunters and regularly hunted two days a week with the South

Oxfordshire hounds. Close beside the stables an unfortunate fox was kept chained up in the Slype, a survival of the old hunting days; he had digged for himself an 'earth' and lived chiefly in that; but a fox is not made for captivity, and he became in his old age a sad and sorry sight; he succumbed at last to the evils of confinement and growing years, his end being hastened, I used to think, by a lampoon written by one of the Fellows upon him.

Spooner's life in New College as an undergraduate is vividly described in the first chapter of his autobiography.

Over the front gate, [he writes] there presided Ring, the Porter whom I have already mentioned. He was an ideal figure for a Porter, being both portly and stately. He was a great gardener, and used to bestow infinite care and pains on the chrysanthemums which grew then, as they grow still, along the Chapel wall and between its buttresses. They flourished greatly under his fostering care and became a notable sight which everyone in the October term used to come and look at. Ring was a devoted servant to the Warden and Fellows, but he recognised no other authority and indeed no other superior. When Prince Hassan, son of the Khedive of Egypt, who was resident in Oxford, came on one occasion accompanied by his Tutor to see the Chapel, and asked to be admitted, he was informed by Ring that he had come at an hour at which the Chapel was not open to visitors. 'But this,' urged the Tutor, 'is Prince Hassan, son of the Khedive of Egypt.' 'I have no orders,' was the reply, 'about no princes, but the Chapel cannot be opened till after 1 o'clock'. Part of Ring's duties was to show visitors into their places in Chapel, and woe-betide the lady (for their presence in College Chapel was not very welcome to him) who ventured to disobey his directions and take a seat she was not intended to occupy; he would not allow her to remain in peace till he had ejected her from it and placed her in the seat he had marked out for her.

Another prominent figure of the time was Parker, the old butler of the College. He was a staunch Conservative: 'It can't be done; it never has been done;' was his answer to any request, however reasonable, if it departed in any degree from the regular routine of College life. He was a keen sportsman and used to go snipe shooting in the meadows near the Cherwell, and sometimes for a day's shooting in the College woods; he kept a dog, and one day he was found giving it a good beating before they started. Being remonstrated with he replied, 'He is sure to deserve it before the day is over'.

Our mode of life in College, though not essentially different from, was in some respects simpler than that now lived. We had morning Chapel, as now, at 8 o'clock in winter and 7.30 o'clock in summer, and this we all attended at least four days a week since there was no alternative Roll-call. The service was much longer, indeed on Litany mornings was very long, as a shortened form had not been introduced. Being always an early riser I used to get half-an-hour's work done before Chapel in winter, and an hour or more in summer. This was not an example generally followed, though a few friends joined me in it during one or two Summer Terms. My early rising in the summer caused much solicitude to the excellent servant of the Junior Common Room, who insisted on supplying me with rum and milk to keep off any possible ill effect of the habit, remarking by way of excuse that he had brought up the daughters of Dr Moberly upon it, and that 'they had done very well.' We almost all breakfasted and lunched together in Common Room, lunch for the more economical men being a very frugal meal consisting of bread and cheese, or rarely a chop, with a pint or half a pint of mild beer. We had no afternoon tea but dined at a quarter past six, the hour being chosen to allow the Fellows time to dress after attending Evening Chapel at 5 o'clock. The majority of undergraduates dined, and asked their guests to dine, in Hall, Clubs being still in their infancy. Dinner cost 2/- a head, but on 'strangers' nights' two nights a week, we had an extra course, and it then cost 2/6d. If we had guests in Hall we took them to Common Room after dinner; there was also a 'Common Room', generally more largely attended, on Sundays, but both guests' nights and on Sundays it was over by 9 o'clock. After dinner when not attending the Union or some Society, we generally played a rubber of whist or a game of billiards for an hour, after that the more studious settled down to a cup of tea and to one or two hours of reading and sometimes more.

My chief amusement was boating, and I rowed a good deal both on the Upper and Lower rivers. Boating in those days at New College was a very amateur affair, my first year the College had no boat on the river at all, and though after that we did always manage to maintain a boat, it remained for a good many years almost at the bottom of the river. To make up for this, we got a good deal of enjoyment out of the unorganised rowing which we vigorously pursued. We had all sorts of College races in which the veriest duffer could take a part, and I still look with pride and pleasure on various pots and cups which I won in them. My proudest moment in these aquatic exercises was when, being admitted to row Bow in the College Torpids, we succeeded in making a 'bump', the delightful sensations at that moment I still treasure up. During the latter part of my time as an undergraduate, we used to make up Fours in College to row down to Sandford or Nuneham; there we often played a game of skittles and got back to College for Chapel and an hour's work before Hall.

Besides rowing, I used often to play 'Fives', and took part occasionally (by special permission) in a game of Winchester Football played in a field in the neighbourhood of the Parks.

It was, Spooner says, 'a very small but not undistinguished society of which I found myself a member when I came up to New College in the autumn of 1862'. Most of the junior members were still, of course, Winchester Scholars. But these, under the recent reforms, were already of improved calibre. There was also a limited number of Choral Scholars, who supplied the men's voices in the College Choir. These Spooner described as 'a valuable element in the community', but this view was not widely shared, and this type of entry was shortly discontinued, 'slain, according to popular belief', writes Spooner, 'by an epigram by one of the Fellows, who applied to the candidates presenting themselves for election a line from the Eclogues of Virgil:—

Nec cantare pares, nec respondere parati
Neither able to sing, nor equal to passing Responsions

a quotation which if not altogether deserved had sufficient truth in it to be the death warrant of the institution'.

The third category of undergraduates was the commoners. These, destined eventually to outnumber all the others, were in 1862 a very small body. Spooner explains why.

The College, [he says] had only lately been thrown open to them; and men from other schools were shy of joining what was still regarded as almost a close Wykehamical corporation. Moreover, a resolution come to by the Fellows when first the College was thrown open to Commoners, of admitting none but those who undertook to read for Honours in a Final School, and the highest standard of the Matriculation Examination which that resolution involved – however well it has on the whole worked in subsequent years – had, for some time at least, the effect of hindering candidates from presenting themselves for Matriculation, and restricted for a good many years the number of Commoners joining the College. But the growth of numbers, if slow, was steady; perhaps all the steadier because it was slow; and popularity, though won but gradually, was at length certainly achieved. By the end of the seventies the number had already grown to something like one hundred and fifty, while before the end of the century, it had reached the full total of two hundred.

The head of this expanding institution, throughout Spooner's time as an undergraduate and as Fellow, was the Rev. J. E. Sewell. Sewell, nicknamed 'The Shirt', is a perhaps extreme exemplification of the unimportance of the Heads of Oxford Colleges. When, rather earlier, Balliol had emerged from its entire insignificance to become one of the leading Oxford Colleges, popular opinion attributed this process to the genius of its great reforming Master, Jowett. Yet when New College went through a similar evolution a few years later, changing from a small, close, Wykehamical corporation of a conservative character to a large, wide-open, liberal-minded and largely non-Wykehamical institution, the Warden was a timid, elderly, conservative Wykehamist who did not actively resist change but did little to promote it. He is chiefly remembered now for the most famous of Oxford's continuity stories. It seems that at the time of the relief of Mafeking in 1899 the bells of every college in Oxford were rung, except those of

New College. The undergraduates came to the Warden to complain of this, to which Sewell replied 'when I was a boy I was walking in the streets of Oxford with my aunt, when they brought to us the news of the battle at Waterloo. The bells of New College were not rung then, and I see no reason to ring them now.' College tradition also attributes to him the comment, on a proposal to instal baths for the undergraduates: 'what do they need baths for? They are only here for eight weeks at a time'. But Spooner took a more benevolent view of the man he described as 'my excellent and revered predecessor in the office of Warden'.

Belonging, [he writes in his second chapter] by birth, sentiment and sympathy, to the older generation of Wykehamists, the friend and schoolfellow of Chief Justice Erle, Lord Hatherley and Lord Selborne, he had served the College, first as Tutor, then as Bursar, and finally two years before my election as Scholar, as Warden. As Tutor he had lectured on Tacitus; as Bursar he had acquired that intimate knowledge of the affairs of the College and of the details of the College property, which, till the day of his death, he invariably exhibited. Coming of a distinguished family, various members of which exhibited exceptional ability, and others those erratic qualities which seem so often to accompany ability, he had, while not himself possessed of exceptional powers, a grasp and command of detail, a gift of methodical and sustained research, of exact and orderly arrangement, of accuracy and thoroughness, which, could he have been induced to publish more, must have won him a high place among the antiquaries of his time. He not only loved the past, but he knew it; and knew it for certain periods and in some of its aspects and details with a thoroughness and completeness which made it live and breathe again. What a delight it was to some of us to listen to some of his more happy speeches at Gaude, when, as it was once pithily put by one of his audience, he seemed to be delivering us a message which came straight from William of Wykeham himself, delivered perhaps from his very deathbed. His style, admirably embodied in his handwriting, was singularly happy and precise; and few were capable of turning off a letter on some important or ceremonial occasion, more neatly and suitably expressed. Of his private character and virtues it perhaps hardly becomes me to speak, but he not only exhibited in all money matters a punctilious and scrupulous honour which was beyond praise, a fidelity to his family, sometimes under trying circumstances, which could not but command respect, but at one supreme crisis of his life he performed an act of self-sacrificing generosity, apparently without question, and certainly without grudging or complaint, to which I know scarcely a parallel. Men might question the necessity of the act or its wisdom; for the self-sacrificing temper displayed in it, nothing but admiration could be felt.* Tradition said that Dr Sewell has been chosen Warden as a compromise candidate accepted both by those who wished for a more advanced reformer and those who favoured a more conservative choice: certainly a chief better suited to conduct the College through a period of active change and progress it would have been difficult to find. Himself conservative by constitution, and averse to change, he yet exhibited unswerving loyalty

---

*Spooner does not identify this 'act of self-sacrificing generosity', but it may be conjectured that it refers to the tangled affairs of Warden Sewell's brother, William Sewell, the founder and later Warden of Radley, who at one time was obliged to flee abroad to avoid his creditors.

The Sewells were an interesting family. Another brother was Henry Sewell, the first Premier of New Zealand, and Elizabeth Sewell, the authoress, was a sister.

to changes if passed by legitimate authority; and carefully carried out and worked the altered state of things not only with conspicuous fairness and good faith, but sometimes, I used to think, with an almost pedantic logic as to the consequences involved. A single instance will serve to illustrate this. New College, in common with most of the other Colleges, resolved, at or about the time of the passing of the Act for the abolition of tests, to abandon compulsory attendance at Chapel on week-days, while retaining it for members of the Church of England on Sundays. The change Sewell disliked, but as usual loyally accepted; but whereas most other Colleges made some reservation requiring men to appear in Chapel on the first and possibly on the last day of Term, and on a few other occasions of general or public interest, at New College the Warden made no such exceptions, but pushed the principle to its full and logical consequences. Thus, while not himself an author of change, he facilitated what he had not originated and did not always approve, and in this way contributed in no small measure to the successful working of the new state of things which he saw gradually growing up and taking shape under his long continued and prosperous rule. A certain simple dignity, old-fashioned courtesy and genuine kindness of heart also greatly endeared him to those who were called upon to work under him and with him, and contributed in no small measure to the successful working of the College, which was conspicuous, in spite of some sharp difference of opinion, for the harmony and good fellowship subsisting among its Fellows.

The Warden being, in spite of Spooner's encomium, a basically insignificant figure, it was to the Fellows that the College owed its remarkable and rapid renaissance in these years. The Fellows of Oxford Colleges were, at this time, changing their function. Teaching undergraduates had not hitherto been thought to be a necessary part of their duties. Many of them were non-resident, and even if they lived in Oxford most of them did not teach. This was all the more inexcusable at New College since the Founder's Statutes, five centuries before, had instituted a system of tuition of the junior members of his College by the seniors which clearly contained the germ of the Oxford tutorial system. But this, like so much else that was good in the Founder's intentions, had been neglected or perverted over the centuries, and at New College, as elsewhere in the University, most of the teaching that undergraduates got came, until the mid-nineteenth century reforms, from private tutors outside the College. Some of these still existed in Spooner's undergraduate days, among them Caird, later Professor at Glasgow and Master of Balliol. Spooner observes that the work done by these 'Coaches', owing to the keeness of the competition among them to obtain pupils, 'was, if not very deep, thorough and well mastered: and the men, feeling that they were paying for their private Tutor, were anxious to gain from him the kind of help they really needed. So they stated their difficulties and perplexities with a fullness and frankness which a College Tutor cannot always secure'. But obviously once the reforms had established that it was the duty of Fellows to teach, the days of the private tutors were numbered.

When Spooner came up to Oxford, New College still contained a considerable number of non-teaching Fellows elected under the old dispensation. Characteristically, Spooner judges them charitably. It is true, he admits, that they did not take much part in the teaching of the College, nor were they generally resident;

but they attended College meetings and at them intervened sometimes actively in its concerns. Their
presence at the meetings was apt to be deprecated and
even resented by the more ardent reformers; and, no
doubt, they often stood in the way and obstructed
reforms which might be urgently needed. Yet on the
whole, their presence in the meetings was probably
beneficial. They prevented changes being made without due consideration, and secured that continuity
between the life of the past and the life of the present
which must always be one of the most valued possessions of an ancient foundation.

What with these dead-weights, and a very conservative
Warden, it is perhaps surprising that the College emerged
at all from its centennial slumbers, from that 'degrading
fate' of which Macaulay writes. That it in fact did so,
rapidly and successfully, was due entirely to another class of
Fellows who were not only active reformers but also
inspiring teachers, and who were thus able not only to
transform the College but to attract to it increasing numbers of able undergraduates desirous of being taught by
them.

Spooner had some tuition from Caird and read essays to
Jowett, but even in his time, so soon after the imposition of
the reforms, his main teaching was from Fellows of the
College, from men like Fearon, later Headmaster of Win-
chester, and from the two great reformers of New College,
Edward Wickham, a Wykehamist and scholar of New
College, later Master of Wellington College and Dean of
Durham, who organised the College's tuition, and Alfred
Robinson, a Marlburian and former scholar of University
College, who became New College's all-powerful Bursar
in later years. Of Wickham Spooner writes that 'under a

cold and almost chilling manner, he concealed great kindness and warmth of disposition.' He was married to Gladstone's daughter and shared the political views of his father-in-law. Spooner considered Robinson 'among the most remarkable characters it has been my fortune to know'. Spooner says of him that

> To those of us who knew him well, and even to the undergraduates generally, he became a sort of external conscience or final court of appeal in matters of conduct, which, had we wished it, we should have found ourselves unable to ignore, and which we hardly ever questioned. Some found the ever present pressure of such a personality, exerting itself as time went on with ever increasing force, as irksome, or even in a few cases, intolerable: but most of us lived under his predominance with a sense of security and confidence which it would have been very difficult to disturb.

But even Spooner himself clashed once at least with this formidable force; his diary for 1882 reveals that 'on Monday I had a disagreeable interview with Robinson having put him out very much by not being strict enough in working the rule as to strangers in Hall on Sunday. This row with him rather put me out in my college work and I have got behind hand in it.' Another Fellow of the College in Spooner's early days was Dr Mayo, the tutor in Medicine, who, Spooner tells us,

> was a very competent doctor, and in pursuit of his profession travelled widely and gained much experience. He served with distinction with the armies of the North in the American Civil War, and made many friends among the Federal leaders. I remember meeting General Sherman as his guest in New College on one occasion and being much struck by his energy,

alertness and perfect frankness. He talked freely about
the War and its incidents without boastfulness, but
also without any mock modesty as to his own achievements.

Mayo was evidently a restless man; in 1877 he left for the
South Seas, taking one of the younger College servants
with him as his valet, and died at sea, of measles, off Fiji.

These were only some of the remarkable men who, as
Spooner arrived at New College, were simultaneously
transforming the College and teaching the new generation
of undergraduates. Spooner describes the work he did as
their pupil in the second chapter of his autobiography:

It was under them that I mainly worked for 'Greats'
or the Final Classical School, and of my reading for
that School, and of what I learnt from that reading,
and from the help and guidance they gave me in it, I
shall now proceed to speak.

Our reading for that School was in some ways
narrower and more restricted, in other respects wider
and more complete than that usually followed to-day.
On one hand our knowledge of the Books we offered,
Herodotus and Thucydides, the *Republic* and the
Ethics, Livy and Tacitus, Aristotle's *Logic*, and Bacon,
and of the great Commentaries on them, Grote's
History of Greece, Mommsen's and Merivale's *Histories
of Rome*, Stallbaum on Plato and Sir Alexander Grant
on the *Ethics*, – was it seems to me much more systematic and complete than anything which is attempted
now. To them we added a rather careful study of the
Pre-Socratic Philosophers (Jowett's great hobby at
that time), a knowledge of the general History of
Philosophy as set forth by Schwegler as well as a
speaking acquaintance with Kant's *Critique* and
Hegel's *Philosophy of History*. Our Logic we worked
at principally in Mill which many of us knew with

SCHOLAR OF NEW COLLEGE

great thoroughness, supplementing it on the critical side by reading his work on Hamilton, Mansel's *Prolegomena Logica* and his appendix on Aldridge's *Logic*; and Ferrier's *Institutes of Metaphysics*. On Ethics we read besides Butler's Sermons, which we knew well, Mackintosh, Mill's *Utilitarianism* and a few of the earlier English moralists, such as Price and Adam Smith, and Jouffroy either in French or English. Our Political Philosophy we studied in Hobbes, in Locke, in Maine's *Ancient Law*, and to some extent in Guizot. Very few of us were specialists according to the modern standard either in History or Philosophy, but we gained from our reading an exceedingly complete view of ancient thought and civilisation regarded as a whole, to which few of the modern generation, who are all more or less specialists, attain. On the other hand, the modern generation both probes more deeply into and reads more widely on the problems of philosophy than any of us were able to do; and if they have most of them lost somewhat their sense of proportion, they are more impressed than we were with the duty of each scholar contributing something, in the line which he adopts as his own, to the advancement of human knowledge. In the statement and apprehension of the ultimate problems of philosophy an advance has been made since our time. I do not feel sure that the fundamental problems are really more grasped than they were by us, but many fresh theories have been put forward and much acute criticism has been expended upon them, and with these the modern student possesses a fuller acquaintance than we from the nature of the case could have; but whether these speculations have thrown much additional light on the ultimate nature of reality seems to me at least doubtful. On the whole, while the problems with which we are confronted and for which we seek a solution remain the same, the centre of interest has to some extent shifted. Fifty years ago, men, under the guidance and prevailing influence of Mill, were asking themselves what is the nature of knowledge, and how have we built up and come by the knowledge which we believe that we possess? To-day our primary question is – what is the nature of that reality which in the last resort our knowledge apprehends or is at any rate relative to? Probably both questions are insoluble; and yet it is certain that the human mind, while thought remains active, will always speculate on them, and speculate, if with but little progress, with some profit; knowledge meanwhile will go on increasing in different directions, and by its increase will at once add to the number of problems to be solved and also suggest fresh directions in which the solution of them may be found.

In History an enormously wider field has been opened up in the past fifty years. Classical archaeology then hardly existed, or was quite in its infancy. The ancient civilisation of Crete, with all the problems which have risen out of its discovery, was still a sealed book and Schliemann's discoveries at Mycenae and Troy were only just beginning to be made. In Roman History again, Mommsen ruled with an authority which, if subsequent discovery and research has done little to upset, it has done much to qualify and supplement. Maine's *Ancient Law* we received with a faith and reverence which the freshness of its methods and the perspicuity of its style did much to justify; and if these are no longer accorded to it in equal degree, it is because fresh results have been reached and fresh enquiries have been conducted by methods and along lines which that great book itself suggested. The method remains, but more facts and more speculations have now to be taken into account. All the questions of comparative anthropology, for so many of which it furnished the starting point, questions such as the priority of patriarchal or matriarchal government, of the origin and growth of private property, of the village community and of tribal organisation, were still quite in their infancy, if not altogether unknown. Yet for most of us, the reading of Maine made an epoch in our mental history, and his *Ancient Law* suggested thoughts and ways of looking at things which remain with us as permanent possessions.

One other point deserves, perhaps, a word of notice. Hegelianism had already begun to be much in the air. In two points in particular it affected us most, in the view which we took of the *History of Philosophy*, and of the *Philosophy of History*. Under the former head we learnt to regard the history of human thought as a drama continuously evolved, each age first by way of reaction and then by way of synthesis carrying on the thought of that which had preceded it, and so handing on the problem in a new shape for solution by the age which followed, different nations no less than different epochs taking a hand in the evolution of truth or of truths, in which all were equally concerned. In the sphere of History again, we found in Hegel's *Philosophy of History* a useful foil to the purely materialistic conception of the evolution of History which had been set forth by Mr Buckle in his *History of Civilisation*. Ideas, we learnt to see, specially as exemplified in such a book as Mr Bryce's *Holy Roman Empire*, exercised a real power in moulding history, no less than the material forces on which Mr Buckle had insisted; and we learnt to recognise that if civilisation in its earlier stages was mainly determined by the material conditions amid which it arose, as time went on, it was increasingly affected by the thoughts and ideals which nations, and still more the great men who from time to time directed their thoughts and aspirations, successively evolved. Further than this we could not go. When we came to consider in detail the formal way in which Hegel attempted to work out his theories, those theories, however ingenious, proved in the last resort incredible. We admired them but we could not believe them or regard them as real representations of truth.

From describing his own life in New College, Spooner in his autobiography proceeds to a general account of the University as a whole. The reader may have already observed that he is inclined to repetitiousness, and that he tends to use a considerable number of words to convey a fairly simple idea. Nevertheless it seems worthwhile to print some fairly extended quotations from his third chapter here, both for their intrinsic interest and for the light they shed on Spooner himself. Interpretation here is not always easy; Spooner tends to jump from his undergraduate days to the Edwardian date at which he is writing, and back again, without always marking the transitions very clearly; the tendency to a certain confusion of thought, a point to which we shall have to return, is here in evidence.

From 1862 to 1870, [he writes,] the University probably touched the high water mark of intellectual activity and eminence. The throwing all Scholarships, and indeed all endowments, open to general competition, though not perhaps altogether favourable to learning, had stirred among all the more ambitious and able undergraduates a feverish kind of intellectual life, and the extension of appointment by open competition in the Civil Service then recently instituted, tended in the same direction. Everything seemed open to a young man of ability coming up to Oxford or Cambridge, Scholarships, Fellowships, great posts in the Civil Service. Learning, then somewhat at a discount, has greatly advanced since, but intellectual activity and hopefulness have diminished.

Of the non-academic side of Oxford he writes at some length:

Outside the Lecture Room intellectual life and interest centred at that time very much in the Union. There were of course College Essay and Debating Societies and Political Clubs, specially the Canning, but they were much less organised and numerous than they have since become; social Clubs scarcely existed; and so the Union bulked larger. It was not as much patronised in New College as in most other Colleges, owing to the existence of the Junior Common Room, which supplied all we needed in the way of newspapers and periodicals. But Dr Fearon was President in my second year and secured me a place on the Standing Committee; so I saw a good deal of the life of the place. Those were, I think, palmy days of the Union, – perhaps one's own undergraduate days are always the palmy days of an institution to which one belongs; they ought to be; 'and the past will always win a glory from its being far'. But they were great days for all that. The preceding days, when Bowen, Bryce and Dicey were the protagonists, had established a great tradition and set a great example. This had been followed up in our generation, when Alfred Robinson, Courtney Ilbert and Richard Robinson of Worcester on the Liberal side, faced Jeune, afterwards Sir Francis Jeune, Phillimore, now Sir Walter Phillimore, and the present Bishop of Winchester on the Conservative. It was an equal fight, for though I thought in those days that the Liberals had the best of it in argument, the Conservatives had decidedly the best of it when it came to voting. This supcriority they retained till within the last few years, when the feeling of the mass of undergraduates seems to have changed, and the vote of the Union has been more often Liberal than Conservative. Perhaps I may be allowed here to observe that success at the Union has been a surer indication of the probability of success in after-life than any other test that has been devised. When in the seventies the Union celebrated its Jubilee, there was an extraordinary gathering of past Presidents; and the number of those who, having held that office, obtained distinction subsequently, was surprising. Indeed it is hardly too much to say that there was scarcely one ex-President who had not obtained some distinction, while many of them had attained to the highest possible positions.

In some respects the social habits of the University have changed since the sixties; I do not now speak of the growth of the married and mixed society which has sprung up around or in connection with the University – of that I shall say more in a later chapter – but the habits and customs of the undergraduates themselves have been modified. In the first place we were by no means to the same extent under the tyranny of athleticism and games as is the present generation. Long walks and short walks were taken as a form of exercise by both seniors and juniors to an extent which would now seem scarcely credible. In the case of seniors, golf was still undiscovered, and remained so till well into the nineties; and the afternoons were not taken up nearly so much as they are now by Committees and Meetings of all kinds, so we took walks sometimes singly, more often two or three together, in all directions, and explored thoroughly on foot the environs of Oxford. On Sundays when we had more time longer expeditions were planned, and a 'Sunday grind' would often carry us, as it does occasionally Dons and undergraduates still, into the Downs of Berkshire and the remoter hills of Oxfordshire and Buckinghamshire. Football was then comparatively unknown; there took place on one or possibly two days a week, an Eton game, a Harrow game and a Winchester game; but they were of the most informal and unscientific kind, and we did not gather, and should have thought scorn to gather, a crowd of lounging, critical spectators to watch us. Fives, on the other hand, and Racquets were more diligently played than at present; at least the absolute neglect of Racquets and the comparative neglect of Fives Courts in Oxford at the present time point in that direction. Boating was perhaps more popular, but certainly less scientific than it is to-day. There were fewer boats on the river, and what there were were probably not as fast as the best in recent years; – sliding seats had not been invented; but men, then as now, worked hard, and the races were as keenly contested as they are to-day. The Cherwell again though occasional punts were to be seen upon it, was far less frequented than at present; indeed it was far less delightful before the new drainage scheme had purified its waters. Sunday punting on the Cherwell and Sunday picnics to Nuneham, were alike unknown, and both would have been accounted 'bad form'. The change in fashion has been mainly due to the influence which London has exercised upon Oxford, and is one of many signs of a lessened self-restraint and a lowered sense of propriety which have become conspicuous in the interval. Cricket was in the Summer Term even more predominant that it is at present, but was carried on under very different conditions. The cricket fields were all on Cowley Marsh; the University ground, known as the Magdalen ground, about a mile from the town, the College grounds some half-mile further on. As there were in those days neither tramcars nor bicycles, the cricket teams used to drive up in four-horse coaches or in hansoms, and lunch was taken on the ground. The coaches were, of course, often driven by some enterprising undergraduate, if he could persuade the legitimate coachman and his companions to let him have the command of the reins. Funny incidents sometimes occurred. On one occasion a well known Don had taken his seat on one of the coaches when an undergraduate proposed to drive it down into the town. The Don objected to the change of coachmen – 'If you are afraid, sir, you can get down', urged the undergraduate: 'But I am the Proctor', answered the Don; 'In that case *I* had better get down', was the ready reply, and so he did. The lunches were not always very orderly nor very sober, more was taken at them than was good for the cricket or good for the men, and the luncheons and drives were a considerable source of expense. In these respects, the more modern state of things where each College has a ground of its own, not far removed from the College buildings, has been a decided improvement on the old.

One change which has occurred in social customs has not, I think been of advantage; besides breakfast parties and luncheons, which still continue, the common form of hospitality in my undergraduate days was to ask one or two friends to dine with you in Hall. At some Colleges, special guest tables where rather a better dinner was served, were provided; at others there were special stranger or guests' nights, at which a better and rather more expensive dinner was allowed: the latter was the case at New College. After dinner you gave your friends a glass or two of wine in your own rooms or in Common Room. It was a pleasant and rational form of entertainment which has now entirely or almost entirely ceased to exist. Dinner in Hall has come to be looked down upon; and indeed when everyone leaves the table as soon as he has finished his own dinner instead of waiting for the whole table to finish, as was the custom in our day, and then rising together, dinner is not a very edifying ceremony. To-day if any one wishes to entertain his friends at dinner, he gives it at a Club or in an Hotel. This is expensive in any case; and as such dinners are usually given to mark a birthday or coming of age, or some other considerable event in a man's life, an expensive dinner is ordered and a good deal of champagne is drunk at it, this leads to extravagance. At the same time, since the guests invited are usually restricted to a little circle of 'intimates' whom the host meets every day, the hospitality becomes narrow and serves a less useful purpose than under the older custom, when one often invited an acquaintance, or friend in the making, instead of one's intimates.

I shall touch on two other questions before closing this Chapter. Have undergraduates become more temperate? and have they become more frugal than they were fifty years ago? As to temperance, I believe that there has been a real advance; both drinking and drunkenness are rarer than they used to be. At private dinners the undergraduate is as a rule very abstemious, he drinks scarcely anything, and even after dinner he is so anxious to smoke that there is very little wine consumed. On the other hand the occasions of a public or a quasi-public kind, such as bump suppers and other similar festivities and coming of age parties, at which some drinking takes place, have multiplied; on these occasions men are apt to let themselves go, and to take more than is wise or right. This is a feature in our modern life which specially needs watching. The habit also of taking whiskey and sodas late at night is perhaps more common than it used to be, and as a man easily falls into taking more than he knows or suspects, the custom is one which calls for vigilance and care. With respect to frugality, my impression is that the general scale of allowances has gone up with the growth of wealth in the country; there are more undergraduates with an allowance of £300 a year and upwards, than there were fifty years ago. The Rhodes

Scholars whose Scholarships amount to £300 a year
are often classed with those who have a large allowance, but this is a mistake. Rhodes Scholars have either
to keep themselves in the Vacations, which can
scarcely be done for less than £100 a year, or to incur
the expense of a long journey home; their allowance
therefore amounts to no more than £200 a year to
cover all the expenses of the Term, and this, as they are
expected to take their full part in games and social
entertainments, is not an excessive amount. With the
increased allowances the scale of expenditure for the
richer men has undoubtedly advanced; a quite absurd
amount in particular is spent on careering about the
country in motors and on motor-bicycles, a sign and a
consequence of the restlessness and love of change
which are so marked a feature of our time. Besides the
almost daily runs which are taken, often to a considerable distance, it is rare to find a man who does not
expect to be allowed to get away once for a change in
the short Term of eight weeks, and a large percentage
of a man's income is thus spent on the means of loco-
motion, or on change of scene, which in a quieter time
would have been thought quite unnecessary. On the
other hand, much less is spent on the niceties of dress
(which are now, as Mr Gladstone remarked, almost
scandalously neglected), on expensive furniture and
perhaps on books and works of art, than used to be the
case, and this, I think, is a misfortune. The throwing
open of College libraries and the multiplication of
libraries of different kinds for undergraduates, which
has marked the last fifty years, though such move-
ments have their good side, have certainly tended to
diminish the desire of the ordinary undergraduate to
possess books of his own, and in this way have pre-
judicially diverted his expenditure into less worthy
channels. On one point everyone is agreed, that the
undergraduate of to-day looks more sharply after his

money than did his predecessor of fifty years ago, and is more keen to see that he gets full value for what he spends.

But if the number of the rich has grown, the number of the poor and struggling has increased at least in equal proportion. Every College contains men who live with the greatest frugality and economy; some Colleges contain a very large number of such men, and all Colleges make it a point of conscience to keep considerable funds to assist men in their struggles. It would not be an exaggeration to say that any man of proved industry and ability coming to Oxford the gainer of a Scholarship or an Exhibition would be enabled to carry through his University course with the assistance which he could obtain from his College or elsewhere. County Councils and other educational authorities often contribute largely, though not always judiciously, to enable deserving students to come to the Universities. If they concentrated their efforts on assisting a smaller number of men of marked character and ability to complete their University career, and made their assistance more adequate, they would probably do more good than by dividing their resources as at present among a larger number of less competent candidates. The Non-collegiate system has also worked, as it was intended to do, in the way of bringing an increased number of poor men to Oxford, some of them pathetically poor; there is a story told in the early days of the movement of a Non-collegiate student being found breaking stones on the road to enable him to eke out his livelihood, so anxious was he to carry through his University course; I am glad to say that when his case was brought under the notice of some of the College authorities, means were found to relieve him from this disagreeable necessity. It must not be supposed, however, that all Non-collegiate students are of this very poor type; they embrace many men of a comparatively advanced age, and others who, for various reasons, are glad to escape the restraints of College life, but come to Oxford, either for the purpose of getting a degree, or to pursue some special branch of study in which they are interested. This is a later development of the system, but such students furnish a valuable and welcome element in our society.

I spoke just now of the growth of facilities for loco-motion as being one cause of the increased expenditure of undergraduates, but it acts also in another way. These facilities bring an ever-increasing number of visitors to Oxford, the numbers passing through during the course of the Summer Term being indeed prodigious. To entertain visitors who are known to him is a real and legitimate source of pleasure to an undergraduate; but it cannot be done without adding, and adding considerably, to his expenditure. Are visitors always as considerate as they should be, in seeing that this item of expense does not fall on those ill able or hardly able to afford it? This same cause has done much to curtail the glories of Commemoration; partly since visitors are now spread over the whole of the latter part of the Term, and certainly come for the 'Eights' even more than for Commemoration itself, the throng which assembles for the latter festivity is in itself diminished; then again, while in earlier days those who came for Commemoration at all came for the whole of it, and passed the greater part of a week at Oxford, at present a large proportion of the visitors come down from London for one, or at most, two Balls, see little of Oxford, and take no part in its festivities except the Balls themselves, and return to London as soon as these are over. Once again, it is a question whether the greater orderliness of the pro-ceedings in the Theatre, in itself from every point of view, a very great advantage, has not done something to detract from the interest of the proceedings for the outside public, and thereby tended to restrict the number of visitors who gather for the occasion. As however, the general scale of magnificence and the consequent cost of tickets at the Balls has increased and the number of those attending them has certainly not diminished, it is at least doubtful whether the undergraduate has been the gainer in point of economy, while the longer period during which the visits of his lady friends and acquaintances are to be expected, has certainly not diminished the expense of entertaining them.

It will be noted that in all this lengthy and highly generalised account of Oxford Spooner has very little to say of himself. He does not even mention that he obtained a First in Classical Honour Moderations in 1864. He does mention his First in Greats in 1866, and this is the opening of a new chapter in his life and in his autobiography.

CHAPTER III

Fellow of New College

SPOONER HEADED THE fourth chapter of his autobiography 'Religious, Intellectual and Social Life in Oxford in
the early days of my Fellowship'. This chapter, the last
which he had typed out, begins with an account of his
final examination as an undergraduate.

I attained a First Class in the Final School of *Literae
Humaniores*, i.e. Classics, in December 1866, my
examiners being Dr Ince, Professor Wilson, Mr
Reynolds of Brasenose, Mr Thorley of Wadham.
The examination still took place in the Old Schools
under the Bodleian Library, in dark and unwarmed
rooms. Being short-sighted, I had to apply for a
special place to be assigned to me near a window. This
was kindly done; but the nearness of the window,
while it gave me more light, brought also an access of
cold, and on one or two days I suffered greatly from
this cause. There was a superstition in those days that
no one who had been reading hard could do himself
justice in the Schools without taking some form of
stimulant, or as it was called 'pick-me-up', so,
admonished by my friends, I went to Mr Prior the
chemist, and received from him a pink mixture com-
posed mainly, I think of sal volatile, which almost took
my breath away when I swallowed it but produced

56

so far as I could observe no other effect upon
me at all. Whether it stimulated my powers I am not
able to decide, for I was a good examinee, and since I
knew my subject fairly well rather took pleasure in
writing answers upon it. The viva voce examination I
also enjoy; and I regret the change which is gradually
substituting purely written examination for the mixed
oral and written examination of earlier days. A good
examiner should, I think, be able to form a better
judgment of a man's knowledge, ability and resource
from a mixed oral and written examination than he
can from written papers alone; and to meet a man face
to face makes the relation between examiner and
examinee more human and personal than only to look
over a set of papers can do. I think that some of the
difficulties which seem to beset the choice of competition candidates for the Home, Indian and Colonial
Service by a purely written examination, would be
met, were an element of viva voce introduced into the
examinations held by the Civil Service Commission;
but probably the number of those entering for these
examinations, the number, complexity and variety of
the subjects very properly allowed to be offered, and
the number of examiners who have consequently to
be employed, make any such suggestion impractic-
able. On the other hand, it is easy to see why oral
examinations are falling into disuse. They occupy
much time, they place a greater strain on the examiners, and no doubt there are more men, – and some of
them excellent scholars too – who fail to do themselves
justice in an oral than in a written examination. Professor Bonamy Price, himself a master in the art of
examining orally, when he returned to Oxford used
to deplore the subordinate place which oral examinations had come to take in the early seventies as com-
pared with the prominence given to them in the days
when he himself was examined. Such a change was no

doubt already noticeable, but since then the decay of oral examination has proceeded even more rapidly. In some Schools, viva voce has altogether disappeared, in others it occupies a very subordinate place; even in *Literae Humaniores* where it is still retained, its position is threatened, and there are ardent reformers who desire its total extinction.

The examination for my degree took place as I have already stated in December; and the College resolved to hold an examination for the purpose of filling up one Winchester and one open Fellowship in the following January. At that examination, I and W. M. Hatch were elected. I was placed first in the examination, and since the Winchester Fellowship, for which as having resided for three years as a member of New College, I was qualified, had first to be filled up, I was elected to it; probably the first candidate not educated at Winchester elected to a Winchester Fellowship at New College for a period close upon five hundred years.

For the next year after gaining my Fellowship, I did work with private pupils with fair success, and so obtained a certain amount of experience in teaching; the work I found hard but stimulating. After a little more than a year's interval, I was appointed first to a Lectureship and finally to a Tutorship in College, and continued to serve the College for more than thirty years in these capacities, and for part of the time in that of Dean also.

After this promising beginning of the chapter confusion sets in. Passages are scored out, restored by a 'stet' and then re-written, and alternative versions appear on alternating pages of the two manuscript notebooks described in the Introduction. Extended quotation from these unrevised sections is hardly possible, or indeed fair to Spooner, and it is easy to see why at this point he abandoned the whole enterprise, though here and there nuggets of wisdom can be found among the débris.

The situation which he is struggling to describe is that prevailing between the two University Commissions of the 1850s and the 1870s. Here there were, it is evident, two quite different battles taking place, Jowett, the Master of Balliol, being deeply involved in both. One of these battles was between the survivors of the Oxford Movement, rallying under Pusey after Newman's secession to Rome, and the Liberals, 'Balliol men in particular', as Spooner says, 'and Jowett's pupils above all, [who] were spread far and wide throughout the University, and began, in virtue of their ability and activity, to command a preponderating influence'. The other battle was that, so often described, between Jowett's idea of a university as a training-ground for the service of the State and Mark Pattison's belief that it existed solely for the promotion of learning.

To the first battle two great Victorian buildings stand as monuments, frowning at each other across Parks Road. On the West side is Keble College which, as Spooner says, 'founded in the early seventies as an express counterpoise to the movement for the abolition of tests, soon became in spite of the opposition which its foundation encountered from the more strenuous Liberals, an important and increasingly important, element in University life'. Opposite it stands the University Museum, originally conceived as the home of all Oxford science, with Professorships and other teaching posts, rather divorced from the Colleges, attached to it. Architecturally these two great buildings have, in a sense, got it the wrong way round. The Museum, exemplifying scientific progress, the only contemporary

building which, for a time at least, received the approbation
of Ruskin, is a fairly traditional work, externally a cross
between a Flemish town-hall and a Venetian Gothic palace,
internally a somewhat uneasy marriage between a medi-
aeval double cloister and a Victorian railway station. Keble,
on the other hand, then the stronghold of reaction, is an
entirely original building, quite unlike anything built before
or (happily) since, perversely ugly in detail but tough and
bold in conception. Its style and manner would have been
much more appropriate to Victorian scientists than those
of the relatively traditional Museum building.

Spooner adopted a middle-of-the-road position in these
two battles. 'Men were divided into hostile camps', he
writes, 'who saw little and even knew little of one another;
harsh things were said on both sides, and little of Christian
charity was too often shown. Personally I had many friends
in both camps, and the alienation of one from the other was
a cause of grief to me.' In a paper which he read to the New
College Essay Society in January 1925, after his retirement
('the men, I think, enjoyed it, at least they said they did' he
wrote in his diary), he analyses at length the differing and,
as he admits, incompatible views on University reform
held by Pattison and Jowett and finds good in them both.
Pattison, he thought, had made a great contribution alike to
University reform and to the well being of the Country.
But some of his ideas were both impractical and undesir-
able, and impossible to reconcile with the College system,
to which Spooner was devoted. Here Jowett had his
sympathies. In the battle between the religious and the
Liberals he was inclined to blur the dividing lines. 'The
hostility [to religion] and the scepticism', he writes, 'have
generally, I think, in Oxford proceeded more from the

philosophers than from the men of science', and he recounts
a story which, he says, had great vogue in Oxford at the
time. A man of science, asked by a lady what his religious
beliefs were, answered 'my religious beliefs are those of
every sensible man'. 'But what', asked his questioner, 'are
those beliefs?' 'That', replied the man of science, 'every
sensible man keeps to himself.' Spooner himself, though
sincerely religious, was not a High Church man, and
though his attitude to the natural sciences was, as we have
seen, a little condescending he was anxious that they should
secure their place in Oxford. He was inclined to be critical
of their later developments. The original founders and
leaders of Oxford science, he writes,

> had all been trained in the old Oxford Classical tradi-
> tion and brought to their new tasks that mental
> activity and alertness, which had been the best and
> brightest part of that tradition. Science at Oxford in
> these its earlier years sprang forward by leaps and
> bounds and leavened the whole intellectual life of the
> University in a marked and even surprising fashion.
> If in the later years it has in spite of the greatly in-
> creased number of its Professors failed altogether to
> maintain the position that it then occupied, this has
> been due in my opinion to two principal causes. In the
> first place it has, quite unnecessarily, I think, been
> inclined to isolate its studies from those of the general
> studies of the place, having for many years put barriers
> in the way of those who have had previously a classi-
> cal training and pursued it as far as Honour Modera-
> tions from passing on in their later years into the
> School of Natural Science. Partly the teachers have
> been so anxious to obtain immediate results from
> their students that they have insisted on shutting them
> up even in their years of preliminary study within the

limits of a single science and have consequently failed to give them that grasp of the fundamental principles of the study they adopt and of its fundamental relation to other branches, without which real effective and prolific researches can scarcely be made. The result is that while good useful work has been done in the different schools it has scarcely been of that significance and importance which the earlier history of Science in Oxford led people to hope and expect, nor has the Oxford scientific school succeeded on the whole in keeping pace with Cambridge.

Some of these comments on Oxford science may retain a little contemporary validity. What is not at all contemporary is the bold way in which this non-scientist feels capable of deciding, from his Olympian classical heights, how Oxford scientists should conduct their affairs. Spooner was an essentially modest man, with a quite humble estimate of his own intellectual capacity, but he retained the serene belief of the Greats man that a classical education both equipped and entitled its products to pronounce authoritatively on any subject.

The 1877 Universities Commission did not resolve these battles; indeed, in slightly different forms they still rage. Spooner did not blame the Commissioners for this.

It has been the fashion in Oxford, [he writes] to find great fault with the reforms both for the University and for the Colleges carried through by the Commissioners of 1877. I cannot myself think these censures well deserved. No doubt being on the whole a band of moderate reformers they were inclined to compromise and were unwilling to press principles in any direction to an extreme. Like most reformers inclined to compromise they succeeded in fully satisfying neither party and so fell into disgrace with both.

In some cases they failed to make up their minds
between somewhat incompatible ideas and tried to
combine them in a not satisfactory manner. But
having difficult questions presented to them for solution they set up in all cases a system which worked
and was capable of further adjustment or development. They strengthened the University out of the
resources of the Colleges without destroying the
independence and efficiency of the latter; they so re-
modelled College offices and reformed College
finances that the career of a College Tutor became the
possible life work of an able and conscientious man.
They did not indeed abolish idle or non-residential
Fellowships, but they greatly curtailed them, leaving
no more than was perhaps sufficient to enable poor
men of ability to start in a profession by their help: if
they did not go to the length of securing that endowments should no longer be held by wealthy men they
did secure that some of the endowments of the Colleges should go to poor men and that all might do so,
if the poor men had ability enough to win them, and a
recent return has shown that in the College which has
trusted most absolutely to open competition [he probably means All Souls] the number of the endowments
secured by poor men has been exceptionally large.
This should be borne in mind when complaints are
made that the Commissioners did little or comparatively little to divert to the uses of the poor may fall
into the hands of the rich, or the comparatively well
to do [a certain Spoonerian confusion here]. Under an
open competitive system this, no doubt, may and
sometimes does happen, but on the other hand such a
system does at least secure that it is only poor men of
really good ability, able to hold their own intellectually,
who secure the prizes, and it is only such who [? are]
in a position fully to profit by a regular university
training, which means the giving up of the calling to

which in the natural order of things they would devote themselves [more Spoonerian confusion]. Such men of great ability have from the earliest times to our own day been welcomed and made the most of at the Universities and have contributed and are likely to contribute in the future their full share to the intellectual strength of the country. The system of Tutorial classes of which we shall have something to say later, is intended to meet a different kind of demand and proceeds on different principles.

This passage, taken from one of the manuscript notebooks of autobiography, is I fear typical of unrevised Spooner, diffuse, repetitive, confused and liable to wander from the point, starting from the 1877 Commission and ending up, by an uneasy but unnoticed transition, with Tutorial classes.

While these battles were proceeding in the University as a whole, New College was busy with its own reforms. A system of joint lectures with Balliol was arranged, on Balliol's initiative. This was at first unpopular with Balliol undergraduates, who, so Spooner tells us, as a form of protest hired bath-chairs to convey them to New College, pretending that it was too far to walk or that they did not know where New College was. But the arrangement was the germ of the present system whereby all College lectures are open to all members of the University.

New College was rapidly growing in size, and new buildings were needed. Spooner was not happy with the resulting buildings on Holywell, designed by Sir Gilbert Scott 'then in the height of his fame'. He felt that they

cannot be regarded among his happier efforts; they are formal, ponderous and lacking in spirit. He was not indeed primarily responsible for their inordinate height

making them so disproportionate to the quaint, pretty old street in which they stand. As originally designed by him they were a storey lower, but the first plans seemed lacking in dignity and impressiveness to the Fellows to whom they were submitted; while the addition of a storey was also recommended to some of them by their desire to keep the cost of each set of rooms within a moderate figure. The result however was decidedly unfortunate and the buildings remain a useful acquisition of which posterity will scarcely be proud.

Spooner was less unhappy about Gilbert Scott's other main achievement at New College, the refurbishing of the Chapel. He was critical of the decision to raise the level of the roof, which he thought fatally marred the exterior, though here again he blamed a decision of the Fellows and not Scott, but of the interior he writes that after Scott's alterations 'the Chapel and even more the beautiful Ante-Chapel form a stately and elevating whole, which is hardly equalled in any other building in Oxford or elsewhere'.

CHAPTER IV

Married Life

ONE OF THE WAYS in which the reformers at New College gave a lead to the University as a whole was in the abolition of the requirement of celibacy for the holding of Fellowships, in this respect anticipating the decisions of the 1877 Commission. Spooner himself took early advantage of this. In 1878 he married Frances Wycliffe, the third daughter of Harvey Goodwin, Bishop of Carlisle. Frank, as he called her, he describes in his diary as

> delicate and often not able to do much work, but when she is well and strong she gets through a great deal in a short time. She is very placid, sometimes impassive, but has a sweet good nature, good sense and plenty of determination. She has a very quiet, beautiful face and a singularly sweet smile which lights it all up.

Ethel Burney, who knew Mrs Spooner in her old age, describes her as

> a dignified, composed, very kind, rather portly person, an excellent hostess, and (as I have just heard from a friend who worked with her) a pioneer in a scheme for the rehabilitation of long-term patients in Oxford hospitals, where the doctors were worried by their

depression and boredom. Mrs Spooner immediately set to work to do something about it, and mobilised all the people who could help with classes in embroidery, tapestry work, etc., with surprising success – the men were interested and produced work of really high standard to their great improvement – and the plan was used in many other places.

The Spooners had seven children. The first two died in infancy, and one was an invalid. The only son who grew up, yet another William Spooner, became a successful inventor of industrial machinery and a distinguished collector of water-colours. The eldest daughter to survive, Catharine, married Campbell Dodson, Keeper of Prints at the British Museum. The next daughter, Rosemary, remained unmarried, became a Labour Councillor on the Oxford City Council, played a great part in the organisation of the Oxford hospitals and was an active supporter of Ruskin College, the trade union college of further education in Oxford. She lived for many years in Oxford with her double first cousin, Ruth Spooner, the daughter of Spooner's brother Max* and of Mrs Spooner's sister. The two Miss Spooners became well-known Oxford figures, bicycling up and down Oxford's hills in all weathers. After Rosemary came Ellen, who married Admiral Arthur Murray; one of their daughters, another Rosemary, became the first President of New Hall, Cambridge, and is now (1976) Vice-Chancellor of Cambridge University, the first woman to hold that post.

*This brother became Archdeacon of Maidstone. He had fair hair and he and his albino brother were known respectively as the Golden Spoon and the Silver Spoon. Another of his daughters married W. R. Inge, the Dean of St Paul's.

Among Spooner's manuscript autobiographical fragments is one headed 'Chapter VIII. The growth of the
Married Fellow and Tutor System in Oxford'. Although
admitting that he was not the first New College Fellow to
marry 'still', he writes,

we were among the pioneers of the movement which
the carrying of the new Statutes was soon to make
widespread and important. In settling our plans we
attached importance to being as reasonably near College as circumstances would permit and as a matter of
fact during all my years as a Tutor I hardly ever failed
to attend morning service in Chapel and a fair proportion of evening Chapels as well. The nearness to College made it also possible to begin work in good time
and to treat College as something more than an office
where business had to be transacted. As a matter of fact
after my marriage I gave the same number of lectures
and had almost as many men as I did while I was still
resident in College.

As our principal means of entertainment we selected
to give dinner parties to the men, it had some draw-
backs, prevented us from seeing much of the young
society which was growing up in the neighbourhood
of the Parks and it enabled us to see only a limited
number of men in the term, but it had great advant-
ages, we could ask our own men to meet men from
other Colleges and people from the outside who were
staying with us and we really did in the course of an
evening come to see and know those we entertained.
The dinner parties were supplemented by Sunday
evening parties for the Freshmen which were sometimes laborious and difficult but served a very useful
purpose in making us acquainted with all the men.
Besides our undergraduate dinner parties I dined two
evenings a week at High Table in College so keeping
up with my colleagues resident there.

The Spooners in fact began their married life at No. 10 Keble Road, a house in a tall Victorian Gothic terrace, of white brick with stone dressing, a few hundred yards from New College. In 1883, as their family grew, they moved to No. 11, a larger house next door. Both these houses now (1976) contain various minor off-shoots of the University; they are due for demolition to make way for extensions of the Nuclear Physics Building.

The 'young society which was growing up in the neighbourhood of the Parks', a little further north, was indeed the germ of North Oxford, the residential suburb created to meet the needs of the new class of married Fellows. It is sad that Oxford celibacy lasted as long as it did; if the marriage of Fellows had been allowed a century earlier, what agreeable late-Georgian terraces, squares and crescents we should have seen stretching northward from St Giles. Spooner describes what actually happened in one of his manuscript fragments. After enumerating some of the first married Fellows to appear in Oxford, he writes:

To accommodate all these and an increasing number of families who followed in their train new quarters had to be provided. The Parks, at first restricted to eight acres in the neighbourhood of the Museum, purchased originally as a site of the Museum, had towards the beginning of this period been fortunately by the foresight of Dr Lightfoot backed up by the influence of Jowett, been [sic] largely extended so as to reach almost their existing limits and had been skilfully and tastefully [?laid out]. Round them and to the north of them there was ample unoccupied ground mainly in the possession of St John's College. On some of this directly the Parks were opened houses had been planted and to those originally erected ones at a somewhat greater distance were gradually added as the demand for them arose, till there was gradually formed the vast suburb of red and white houses, which running for a mile or more along both the Banbury and Woodstock Roads and filling the district East and West of them as far as the Cherwell on the one side and Port Meadow on the other, forms such a marked feature of modern Oxford as you approach it from the North. From an architectural point of view I fear that the results must be regarded as on the whole unsatisfactory. The earlier houses put up mainly by speculative builders, were poorly planned and poorly built, being designed for the most part on the villa pattern, common in the suburbs of other growing towns; and though as time has gone on, the stamp of houses and the accommodation provided in them have greatly improved, the houses have never lost the character originally stamped upon them, but have remained predominantly villa residences to the present time, residences which ill fit in or accord with the grey stateliness and the severe simplicity of the earlier college buildings. Nor has the planning of the new suburb been altogether very successful. The streets indeed are mostly wide and spacious and in the glory of the flowering shrubs in the late spring are for a short time exceedingly beautiful; but at other times they present a somewhat mean appearance; the gardens tend generally to be monotonous and undistinguished and the cross streets have for the most part little to recommend them.

Perhaps they seemed less disagreeable in the eighteen-seventies than they did to Spooner writing his autobiography in the reign of King Edward VII. Mrs Humphrey Ward ('he on the staff of Brasenose, she a daughter of

Thomas Arnold, then doing work in Oxford', as Spooner describes them) in *A Writer's Recollections* describes life in North Oxford in a happier light. 'Nobody under the rank of a Head of College, except a few privileged Professors', she tells us, 'possessed as much as a thousand a year. The average income of the new race of married Tutors was not more than half that sum. Yet we all gave dinner parties and furnished our homes with Morris papers, old chests and cabinets and blue pots'. In Liberty gowns they went out to dinner in Bath chairs, the husbands walking. From this kind of life the Spooners were evidently rather aloof, living a little nearer in, entertaining undergraduates rather than other dons, consorting with the higher clergy and not with intellectuals like the Wards. But dons too were occasionally invited; at one of the Spooners' dinners a guest was 'Dodgson (*Alice in Wonderland*). I had a good deal of talk with him partly about the reformation of the drama, partly about harmonies in other scenes besides that of sound. He has a curiously original unexpected sort of mind, always interesting to me'. Various Lewis Carroll figures are thought to have been based on Spooner, but there is no real evidence for this. Dodgson's diaries contain only three brief references to Spooner.* In October 1878 he dined with Sewell, the then Warden of New College, and notes that 'Spooner introduced me to his bride'. On 10 November 1881 he writes 'Dined with the Spooners and met the Talbots'. This is the dinner which Spooner mentions in his diary; Talbot was the Warden of Keble, later Bishop of Winchester. Finally on 5 May 1884 Dodgson writes 'Wrote to Spooner (who had invited me to dine) to beg off on the

*I am grateful to Professor Mortin N. Cohen for calling my attention to these passages.

ground that in my old age I find dinner-parties more and more fatiguing. This is quite a new "departure" – I much grudge giving an evening (even if it were not tiring) to bandying small-talk with dull people.'

It is at about this time that Spooner's autobiography peters out. But in 1881 he begins to keep a diary, and from this point on, intermittently at least, we become much more intimately acquainted with him. The diary has a characteristic exordium.

> I am beginning this, [he writes,] because I forget many things which are interesting and which I should wish to remember and also because I think it may be a pleasure hereafter to myself and to others to look back upon things that I have done and that have happened to me and to read again thoughts that I have thought that may have passed out of mind. I should wish to keep some kind of record of the more remarkable public events that occur in my time and to write down for my future use and benefit such words of others, whether read or heard, as may seem striking or worth remembering. *Quid quid agunt homines nostri est farrago libelli*. I think I may get some advantage from this and that the time spent in writing this book may be not wholly mis-spent.

It was not wholly mis-spent, but the diary hardly lives up to this high promise. Much of it reports fairly trivial family events, and reports them without the vividness that makes the similar diaries of, for instance, Parson Woodforde so enjoyably readable. But its style is certainly an improvement over his other writings. In what he wrote for publication, in *Fifty Years in an Oxford College* and in his published works, his style is orotund and even vapid; one word is never used where five will do. There is a comic example of this in the introduction to his edition of Tacitus's *Histories*, where, needing to paraphrase Tacitus's famous description of Galba as *omnium consensu capax imperii, nisi imperasset*, he writes 'He whom, before he had been emperor, all would have pronounced fit for the post had, when the opportunity came to him, been tried and found wanting' – twenty-seven words to say less than Tacitus had said, better, in six. But in the diaries he is often pithy and pointed. From time to time there are lively and even acid comments (a sermon in the University Church is described as 'a melancholy wail', and after dinner at Magdalen he describes the place as 'much as of old, comfortable but sleepy and uninteresting'), and there are some compelling pen-portraits and some surprisingly frank comments on his own character and achievements. The self-portrait and the portraits of others will be the subject of a later chapter; now we are concerned with the remaining events of Spooner's time as a married Fellow of New College.

Spooner's marriage made a great difference in his life. Mrs Spooner was a powerful character, much attached to her own family, and after his marriage Spooner spent great stretches of his vacations at Rose Castle, the palace of the Bishops of Carlisle. There are faint signs of restiveness about this at first. Mrs Spooner on one occasion refused to go and stay with some of her husband's relations, preferring to stay at Rose, and Spooner recorded his disappointment in his diary, adding 'I feel at times growing so dreadfully out of knowledge of my own kith and kin, as if I never saw them'. But later he writes of the end of a happy visit at Rose, 'sorry, as I always am, to go'. He came more and more to admire his father-in-law, and when the Bishop died in the autumn of 1891 Spooner wrote in his diary that 'life seems dreadfully poorer by his absence and of course the loss of such a home as Rose Castle means a great loss both in our lives and in the lives of the children'. What made it worse was that the Bishop's successor, though 'a good sort of man', was 'not a gentleman'. Spooner was perfectly frank and straightforward about class distinctions; a new Bodley's Librarian appointed in 1882 is also described as 'not quite a gentleman', and when his sister-in-law's nurse falls ill he writes 'We heard that Brown had diphtheria at Maidstone, sad for Kate'.

Rose Castle was of course not the only house where he stayed. He was in fact a fairly assiduous country-house visitor. He describes at some length a visit to Crewe Hall. The third Lord Crewe, to whom it then belonged, was the grandson of Lady Crewe, the famous Regency hostess, and thus the great-grandson of Fulke Greville. He was not himself a man of any great distinction, but his sister married Monckton Milnes, a much more interesting man, later Lord Houghton, who was also staying at Crewe Hall when Spooner was there. Lord Crewe had no heir, and on his death Crewe Hall became the property of Lord Houghton's son, later Marquess of Crewe, the Liberal statesman and diplomat. Crewe Hall now belongs to the Duchy of Lancaster, who have let it on a long lease to a scientific foundation. Spooner's visit there was in September 1883:

Tuesday we went to stay with Lord Crewe at Crewe Hall. We arrived there in company with the Dean of Lichfield and Mrs Bickersteth and found staying in the house the Bishop of Gibraltar, W. Bristowe Vice-Chancellor of the Duchy of Lancaster, his wife and daughter, Lord Houghton, Lord Crewe's brother-in-law, a Mrs Ackers, a neighbouring squiress, W. Skene brother-in-law to the Archbishop of York, Mr & Mrs Clayton, Mr Norwood a neighbouring clergyman. Lord Crewe himself is a curious mixture of ability and the want of it. His mind is narrow but works intensely in the groove in which it runs. He is a master of detail, arranges all the detail of the Household himself. He is a quick observer, but interested almost entirely in questions of law and Theology, most of all in preachers whose respective claims and excellences he is never tired of discussing. He has also a curious memory for classic sayings, which sometimes he brings out unexpectedly. He is pleasantest when the company is small and his mind at ease and then loses something of his restless nervous manner. We saw a good deal of him, as from Friday till Monday we were alone with him except for Mr Malcolm MacColl, except one day when he got upset by some arrangements for a Church opening having gone amiss we found him very pleasant. Lord Houghton I liked, but he made me sad. He has a restless mind and body and is somewhat of a disappointed man. As he says himself, he has tried everything having been up in a baloon [sic] and down a coal-mine and has no fresh interest in life left; so he is fairly blazé [sic], does not know what to do or what to turn to. Vice-Chancellor Bristowe was a very agreeable clever man, talked almost continuously and always well. He has a great fund of accurate information and a very clear way of expressing himself. He took me over the works at Crewe, the manufacture of steel by the Bessamer [sic] process, the making and testing of the springs for engines and carriages, the manufacture of steel sleepers, and the building up of the engines were the four things that interested me most. Miss Bristowe was a modern aesthetic young lady not wanting in ability but sadly wanting in common sense and reality. Mr Skene was a hustling energetic type of

clergyman, inclined to talk about his own achievements, but no ways out of the common. Mr Norwood
was a remarkable man, a fine archaeologist and good
geologist; he had a great knowledge of Shakespeare
and of English poetry generally. He talked well on
every subject not least well on Darwinism. He had a
fresh genial truth loving mind it was a pleasure to
come in contact with. I learnt a good deal (not least
lessons in patience) from him. He thought that a
clergyman's business should be to preach chiefly on
the ten commandments and enforce them with a stick
on weekdays and believed on the whole the clergy
wisely and judiciously did this. The house is a very
fine one; it was burnt and built up by Lord Crewe for
£240,000. The original house, the shell of which is
perfect, is Jacobean. It is square, 100 feet each way.
The centre of the house used to be a small open court,
the corridors looking into which were glazed. In the
restoration this court has been roofed in and the corridors open into it. Thus the house runs round a double
hall, the entrance hall and this narrow larger marble
hall behind. Out of this second hall at the far end
the Chapel opens and sets of rooms on either side. The
great dining room opens out of the first hall. The
Chapel is very beautiful. There are bronze medallions
let into the panels all round and a beautiful reredos
with Mosaic figures at the back of the altar. Lord
Crewe and most of the ladies attend Chapel in a
gallery at the west end. The women servants and all
the lady guests go to Chapel in their bonnets. The
entertaining rooms, the gallery, the drawing room,
the card room and the Library are all at the top of the
house and it is these which give it one of its most
distinctive features. The great gallery is a very fine
room 100 feet long on the north side of the house,
looking over the Italian garden and lake. Here they
breakfast, the guests arranged at two or three separate

tables. There are good family portraits in that room, going back to the time of Elizabeth, but the most precious ones, the Sir Joshua Reynolds, are in the drawing room. One of these has a curious history. Lord Crewe sent it to be cleaned a while back. It was a picture of his grandmother and represented her standing with her arm resting on a tripod table. When the cleaner received [?it] he told Lord Crewe that a piece had been cut out and a new piece inserted and he believed he knew where the missing piece was to be found. Lord Crewe commissioned him to obtain it, if he could, and he obtained from a house in Belgrave Square the missing portion. It was of a boy, an uncle of Lord Crewe's, represented as a Cupid and the tripod table had been merely inserted to fill up the space which the boy had occupied. The genuineness of the recovery was placed beyond doubt not only by the fact that the picture exactly fitted the space which had been filled up, but also because they found a print of the picture with the Cupid boy (and not the table) represented in it. In the gallery besides the pictures are three or four Japanese and French marquetry cabinets and other things of great value. One piece of Dresden china, a ship, bought by Lord Crewe himself for £150 he sold not long since for £5000, the dealer taking it straight off to Paris to one of the Rothchildes [sic]. Towards the end of our time arrived Mr Malcolm MacColl a great friend and protegé of Mr Gladstone. He told us a good many interesting things. . . . I had some talks with Mr MacColl about Mr Gladstone's appointments and policy, both of which he vehemently upholds. I believe that with the appointments W.G. takes great pains. On Sunday I preached for the Schools interesting the congregation but not I think Lord Crewe himself very much. The Sunday was one of the most lovely days I can remember. Our rooms were called the Nantwich rooms on the ground floor –

a little suite to themselves – There are beautiful hot houses, greenhouses and fruit houses of all kinds and a fine garden, But Lord Crewe has no flowers in the house in the country only in Town. He wanted me to go back for Michaelmas Day but I cannot manage it. I took quite a holiday this week; did no work.

Less grand but more frequently recurring visits were to his brother-in-law Max at various Kent parsonages, and to other relations about the country. On one occasion, visiting E. C. Wickham at Wellington College, he found the Master's mother-in-law, Mrs Gladstone, staying there too.

I had a good deal of talk with her, [he records] I think the chief impression she made upon me was that of having a certain unworldliness and a most enthusiastic admiration of her husband. She clearly also much enjoys, but in a frank naive way, his position as Prime Minister. I always lament her slovenliness in dress, her want of savoir faire and of respect for the usages of society. These things though not very important, mar the influence of one in great position.

He is very free with his comments on his fellow-guests. 'He is troubled with the sad infliction of being a bore', he writes of one, and another he describes as 'a pushing self-praising clergyman I did not greatly care for'. At another country house he meets 'a sad young man who seemed to have no taste for anything in particular and resented not having any'. Of one of his own guests in Oxford he writes 'I never like her as much as I expect to; she is bright and clever and very much interested in things but always somehow seems to be pushing some private plan of her own'. On another occasion, visiting Cambridge, he mentions meeting 'the whole of the Cambridge world. That socially, I think, is not equal to ours: it wants a head and some lights to relieve it; rather second-rate and ill dressed but shrewd and intelligent'.

But of course all these visits about the country were peripheral to his main work in Oxford. There he was undoubtedly industrious. 'Greek History, Aristotle's *Logic*, St Mark's Gospel are my Lectures this term', he writes. No one at Oxford in these days would cover so wide a field. He was always uncertain about his lectures, though he worked hard at them; in October 1896 he wrote 'I do not get on with the men' (this is his invariable term for undergraduates) 'in Lectures and do not like Lecturing, as I like taking the men individually'. In 1882 we find him writing 'I was disappointed that the men did not seem more ready to come to my History Lectures; perhaps I do not take pains enough with them'. But next year he has added 'Mods Logic' to his lecture subjects which he now thinks have become 'rather too many – I think the Divinity and Greek History have been decent, the other two feeble.' When later in the year there is a meeting at Balliol about arranging inter-collegiate lectures he writes 'I am rather afraid of being expunged as not a sufficiently good lecturer'.

He was even more hesitant about his sermons. 'I wish I could get for my sermons more power of illustration and anecdote and more variety, they are so apt to be dull', he writes in July 1882, and a year later, preaching for a friend in a country parish, 'it interested him, I daresay the more educated people in the congregation, but I cannot put things simply, vividly, strikingly enough for the uneducated'. 'The sermons, alas!' he writes again, 'are still rather a weariness to me to write. Composition never

79

comes easy and my mind is not very well furnished with Theological ideas nor I fear with Theological Principles.'

Perhaps this is the place to examine Spooner's religious beliefs. He was consecrated Deacon in 1872 and Priest in 1875. Neither of these events is mentioned in his autobiography, and they come too early for his diary, which also fails to allude to his appointment by Bishop Stubbs as an Honorary Canon of Christ Church in 1899, and does so only in passing to his Doctorate of Divinity in 1903. We do not know if his decision to enter the ministry was automatic or the result of deep reflexion, but it was normal, though no longer obligatory, for Fellows of Oxford Colleges in his time. There are one or two illuminating passages in the diary. One Good Friday he writes of the two-hour service

It is always to me rather a painful service. The cry, *Eloi, Eloi Lama Sabachthani* is so like a cry of failure, that it requires Easter and still more the after-history of Christianity to make one feel sure that it was not a failure but the greatest of triumphs. I think that the two arguments for Christianity which have most weight for me are the historical growth of Christianity and the certainty of conviction which its reception inspires in individual Christians.

Elsewhere he writes

I feel that Anglicanism taking it all in all is for Englishmen at any rate the best working hypothesis that has yet been invented. It is less repelling, meagre, unprogressive, unhistorical than Calvinism, more reasonable, liberal and capable of greater progress than Romanism, even if it wants the authority of its pretensions. It finds a place and a meaning for the Sacraments that Calvinism scarcely does. As to confession and discipline I should differ probably from many of its professors and should wish a more representative legislature than they would be ready to accept, yet on the whole I am prepared to work with them, only trying as best I may to shape the Church – while still regarding it as a divinely provided spiritual body, to meet the wants of the time.

In January 1883, he says,

I have felt like Martha lately, cumbered with much serving and choked by the cares of this life. It is hard to be really spiritual I find, even in my prayers. Thoughts of the house, of how to provide the money for it, of public affairs will come into my head and interrupt my prayers – my very lectures do so at times – till I feel sometimes as if I were no better even for my prayers.

In a letter to Sir Henry Acland of August 26th 1900, shortly before Acland's death, he writes

I am writing this looking out on what always seems to me one of the most beautiful views in England – the view across Grasmere Lake of Silverhow and Lough-rigg, and I cannot help feeling that God, who has made this world so singularly beautiful and has given us such a power of consciously enjoying its beauty, must have in store for us in that world, into which death will bring us, at least equal beauties and an equal power of enjoyment. I quite admit that we cannot be sure of this, that we have to accept it on faith, but this is in accordance with the rule of our lives, we have always to judge of what to expect by what we have already experienced, and though the venture in this case may seem greater than in others, still, since what we have experienced is the only evidence by which to guide ourselves, why not trust that evidence as we do, and are bound to do, in other cases? Remember that here too we are not going against our own instincts but entirely with them. One other thing I will add. God does not expect of us impossibilities; and if we have honestly used such powers and gifts as we have to the best of our ability (and I believe this to be the case with you) the issue of our lives we may safely leave to him. 'That which a man soweth, that shall he also reap'.

Some light is thrown on Spooner's religious position by his correspondence with Hastings Rashdall. Rashdall, who taught history, philosophy and theology at New College from 1895 until, in 1917, he became Dean of Carlisle, had somewhat latitudinarian views on religion. College tradition has it that Spooner, on being asked if there were any Christian Socialists in New College, replied 'Yes, there are two, Rashdall and myself, but I am not much of a Socialist and Rashdall is not much of a Christian'. In April 1914 Rashdall was soliciting signatures for a document produced by the Churchman's Union favouring liberal attitudes in the Church to questions of episcopacy, relations with other denominations and even the Incarnation. Spooner replied 'I think on the whole I prefer not to sign your document. I do not want you to be prosecuted and I am glad you should remain a teacher in the Church, since you honestly feel you can do so; but I cannot go so far as you in questioning the fundamental positions of the Creed and prefer therefore not publicly to associate myself with your body'. But many years earlier, in 1898, he had written of Rashdall, in a testimony supporting his application for the post of preacher at Lincoln's Inn, that 'he always seems to me to combine, perhaps to an unusual degree, real activity of mind with clear and undoubting conviction on points which are truly essential.' Later, in 1910, he congratulated

Rashdall on a sermon and added 'you may yet do much to keep philosophy religious as well as to make religion more rational and philosophical', and he voted for Rashdall as Bampton Lecturer, writing to him afterwards that 'I hope and think your lectures may be a great help to a good many people'. But he did not think Rashdall ought to become a country parson. When Worthen, one of New College's major livings, became vacant, Spooner, after discussing various candidates in a letter to Rashdall, wrote 'Don't go yourself, you would only eat your heart out, attributing all possible misdeeds to the neighbouring squires – which would not do them much good and you much harm.'

Spooner himself, in spite of his doubts about his own preaching abilities, enjoyed taking occasional parish duties. But he clearly took himself more seriously as a teacher than as a priest. He says of Bishop Butler in the book he wrote about him, that 'education meant to him, as it has meant to almost all sensible men, a religious education'. Spooner never seems to have seriously contemplated leaving New College for parochial work. He refused all offers of livings, including, in January 1892, what was then New College's most valuable living, Saham Tony in Norfolk.* As the

*Two years later, Spooner visited Saham Tony and wrote the following rather startling note in his diary. 'The place I thought charming, but the memories of Adams, his wicked ill-spent life and deserted lonely death, was painful and rather haunted me'. Coker Adams, the previous rector, had died on 27 December 1891. He was born in 1827, admitted to New College as Founder's Kin in 1847, and presented to the living of Stockton in 1870 and to that of Saham Tony in 1876. He was the author of several pamphlets on Church doctrine and defence. A report on the Rectory presented to New College on 8 January 1892, ten days after Adams's death, has frequent references to 'the neglect of the late Rector'. The Rural Dean reported that 'at least three-fourths of the population may be described as Dissenters, although he believes that a large proportion of the so-called Dissenters are

writer of his entry in the *DNB* puts it, the College was his parish. Indeed in 1882, at a meeting about religious instruction in the College, he was appointed to undertake it, 'but without prejudice to the rights of the rest; I will do what I can in the matter, but do not expect to be able to alter much from what I do now'. He seems to have had very little to do with the services in New College Chapel, of which he is often critical; he says of the choir at Magdalen that it 'has a finish and perfection – a sense of apparent reverence also, which our New College choir now sadly wants', and of an organist at New College that he 'played carelessly and ill and the whole service was heartless and slack. I was vexed and disappointed'. He was not always so gloomy. A loose sheet inserted in his autobiography gives his views on New College Chapel services.

> Our Musical College at New College a legacy from the original foundation of William of Wykeham of which Choristers and Chaplains formed an integral and important part has proved sometimes a hindrance, sometimes a help in the matter of the attendance at Chapel. On the one hand a certain number of men are attracted to the College by the musical tradition which still pervades the place and by their affection for the musical services which play so important a part in it.

---

not really hostile to the Church, and many would probably return if a suitable and popular incumbent was appointed to the living'. The Rectory was in a condition of great neglect, and the 'Gardens and Pleasure Grounds' are described as being 'in a shocking state, – the Pleasure Grounds have been to a large extent destroyed and the Kitchen and other Gardens are got into a very foul and neglected condition'. It was clear that an incoming incumbent would be involved in heavy expenditure. Perhaps it is not altogether surprising that Spooner, who must have seen this report, should have refused the living. But we shall probably never know what he meant by his reference to Adams's 'wicked ill-spent life'.

On the other hand there are a certain number of men who either positively dislike the musical service or find it formal and unreal and are therefore so far indisposed to attend it. On the whole I think during a series of years the musical service has attracted more than it repelled. It is also necessary to take into account the real service which our College Choir, particularly under the energetic management of Dr Allen* has rendered to the general cause of Church Music in England. Not only has it tended to recall to notice and to general use a good deal of the more ancient Church music which had been forgotten or neglected but yet was well worth preserving, it also gives the younger composers a chance of being heard and appraised under favourable conditions which it would have been otherwise difficult or impossible for them to secure.

Spooner remained a keen sermon-taster, and comments freely in his diary on those he heard. On one occasion he comments that a sermon by Mandell Creighton, then Bishop of Peterborough, was dull, while that of Archbishop Benson next day was 'claptrap'. On another occasion he describes some Bampton Lectures as 'the event of the term' (the Bampton Lectures are actually a series of sermons delivered in the University Church; they still continue but I fear no one now would regard them as the principal event of any term).

Of course his religious responsibilities were not the only ones he held in College. From 1876–1889 he was Dean, the officer responsible for College discipline. In those days the College seems to have been a quiet and orderly place. In 1882 New College went Head of the River for the first time

*Later Sir Hugh Allen, Heather Professor of Music and Director of the Royal College of Music.

which 'was an occasion of great rejoicing. They made a great bonfire in the Garden Quadrangle and danced round it shrieking; when I went to stop them they danced round me but did no mischief'. Even this was an isolated incident. In one of his autobiographical fragments he writes 'the only mistake I made was the retention of my office as Dean when no longer resident in College'. The fragment breaks off here and no explanation of this is offered. He also does not explain why he ceased to be Dean; all he tells us is that at a College meeting in January 1890

> I was appointed Dean of Divinity to make up for my ceasing to be Dean. Professor Sylvester and some of the other Fellows were indignant at the appointment. . . . Matheson succeeded me as Dean and has done well in that capacity, better in some ways than I did. It was, however, a great blow to me parting with the office and I began the term in thoroughly low spirits.

His diary says little about his individual pupils. He had few illusions about them. After one Gaude he comments in his diary 'There was no one of great interest there; indeed I begin to fear that, however excellent the men we turn out, and many of them are very nice, they are rather an undistinctive, undistinguished set'. He seems to have ruled them with a curious mixture of shrewdness and innocence. It is recorded that on one occasion he was asked by an undergraduate pupil for leave to go to Epsom to join a family party on the first Wednesday in June. 'Do you promise that it is to Epsom you would be going?' The promise was given. 'Very well then, you may have leave to go to Epsom – but if you had asked me for leave to go to Derby it would have been refused.' He later became famous for extraordinary insights into the characters and destined careers of members of the College, but the only notable comment he makes in his diaries on a particular pupil is rather wide of the mark. When an undergraduate named Benson only got a pass in Schools he writes 'he has given himself entirely to acting, but I doubt whether he has it in him to become first-rate in that line' and later 'F. Benson is still bent on getting on the stage, but I cannot think he will be a great sweep'. However in October 1896 he goes to see the later Sir Frank Benson as Hamlet and is taken behind the scenes to shake hands. He was quite a keen theatre-goer, records several visits to London plays in which 'Irvine', as he persistently describes him, takes the leading part, but is much shocked by the pantomime at Manchester – 'the songs were simply coarse, made all the coarser by the odious woman who sang them and though some of the scenes were pretty they were spoilt in my eyes by the extreme scantiness of the dresses'.

Like all serious-minded Oxford dons he believed in research as well as teaching. He only published two books. The earlier was his edition of the *Histories of Tacitus*, published in 1891. This was well received at the time, and since no comparable critical edition of the *Histories* has appeared subsequently in English it still holds the field. But it hardly stands comparison with Furneaux's edition of the *Annals* (in his introduction Spooner writes 'Had I, when I commenced the work, known that an edition by Mr Furneaux might ultimately be looked for, I should not have ventured to undertake it, feeling how unequal to his are my qualifications for the task'); it lacks historical sense and has his characteristic defect of verbosity. But when, about a year after its publication, he was elected to the Athenaeum, he records that 'my Tacitus rather helped me'.

His second major publication was a little book about Bishop Butler. This was published in 1901. It made little mark at the time, and I doubt whether anyone has looked into it much since. I am told by those better qualified to judge than I am that, though rather thin and lightweight, it is not in any sense ridiculous in its approach to Butler's philosophy. The 'Life and Times' section is competently done, and Spooner disposes, it seems to me effectively, of the rather absurd rumour that Butler shortly before his death was received into the Roman Church.

These two books do not exhaust the list of Spooner's writings for publication. He contributed a laudatory article on William of Wykeham to a series entitled *Typical English Churchmen* published by the Society for the Promotion of Christian Knowledge (the Society had earlier much annoyed him by rejecting what he calls 'my Political Economy' – this does not appear to have survived). He was also for some years Oxford correspondent of *The Guardian*. This was of course not the Manchester newspaper but an ecclesiastical weekly, now defunct. In September 1892 he received what he called 'a great blow', when Lathbury, the editor, wrote to tell him he did not wish him to continue to act as Oxford correspondent; 'as the work interested me and kept me in touch with the outside world I was greatly grieved. I have practically done nothing in the way of writing for the paper since – which I regret'.

Whatever the merits or demerits of Spooner's writings he himself was under no illusions about his own position in the world of learning. One day in 1882 he went for a walk with Margoliouth, newly elected a Fellow of New College and later to be the immensely distinguished Laudian Professor of Arabic; a little wistfully Spooner records that

Margoliouth 'lets one see something into that confraternity which there is among really learned men'.

All the same, Spooner was a many-sided man. In addition to his religious activities, his teaching, his lecturing on a wide variety of subjects, his writings, his social life and country-house visiting, he was very active in good works. In the abortive Chapter V (re-numbered IV) of his autobiography he writes 'As an undergraduate I had already taken a small part in social and Philanthropic work. Beggars always appealed to my imagination; they seemed to lie so much outside the regular social order, to live such an unsatisfactory, aimless, hopeless life.' The subsequent paragraphs are scored through, but it is apparent that he joined something called 'The Anti-Mendicity Society', later renamed 'The Charity Organisation Society'. In the latter he evidently played a prominent part; his diary is full of references to attendance at its meetings, including troubles with a defaulting Treasurer. He was a Poor Law Guardian, and much concerned with a Workhouse School. He was on the Council of Oxford House, the University Mission in Bethnal Green.

Nor were these his only activities outside New College. He was for many years on the Council of Lady Margaret Hall, and helped this, the first founded of the Oxford women's Colleges, in its earliest days, becoming Chairman in 1901. Though he worked hard at this, his diary records that 'I find myself much out of sympathy with the more go-ahead party in the women's education movement', and he was opposed to the admission of women to degrees. In the summer of 1895 there was what he calls an 'agitation' in favour of this; 'I joined and took a more or less leading part in the Committee which was formed to oppose the movement'. It was rejected by a large majority of Congregation in the following summer.

Another of his outside activities was the Political Economy Club, of which he was for many years Secretary. His diary mentions regular meetings of this Club, but without indicating his own views on any of the topics discussed. In politics he began as a Liberal, but gravitated towards the Conservatives, influenced it seems mainly by a dislike of Mr Gladstone's Irish policy; towards the close of 1881 he wrote in his diary 'In politics I have drifted away more from the Government, viewing the Irish Land Bill with special dissatisfaction'. He seems to have remained a fairly mild Conservative; he mentions a visit to the Rector of Ludlow 'such a virulent Conservative that he nearly reconverted me to be a Liberal'. No such reconversion occurred, however; in April 1891 he records that 'Willie Benson came to stay with me on Saturday to help his brother who was the Gladstonian candidate for Mid-Oxfordshire. I was glad to have him to stay with me, but glad also that Geoffrey Benson was not successful, Mr Morrell was returned'. Spooner's previously mentioned flirtation with Christian Socialism seems to have been a very mild one. His diary records that in March 1892 he read a paper on 'the Principles and Practice of the Poor Law' to the Christian Social Union; 'The Union has socialistic leanings but received my paper tolerantly and kindly. I agreed to become a member of the Union'. But his diary never mentions it again, until in May 1905 he read a paper to it on 'The Choice of a Profession'.

Spooner was also mildly conservative in University affairs. His diary of 1893 records that 'the resolution in favour of the foundation of an English School passed

December 5. I am not myself in favour of it and was sorry it passed'. Later, in an entry for May 1894, he writes

> There has been a good deal of debate lately about the establishment of a School of English Literature and Language. The proposal was carried in a Congregation held on Tuesday May 1. I am against it both because, I think, it is not a good subject to examine in, because I believe it to have been carried in the interests of the women and not of the men and also because I desire to keep some fields still free from the influence of the Examination system.

The next year he writes 'I also did something to prevent Anthropology being made a subject for a separate Final School, which made the natural science people very angry.* In October 1896 he writes

> The University settled to have an examination and grant a diploma in the art of teaching, and has made some arrangements for having the art taught. The radicals are rather keen upon the plan and I did not object, though I do not feel hopeful of its doing much

---

*In a long apologetic letter to Sir Henry Acland (on May 28th 1895) Spooner said that his main reason for his opposition to Anthropology as a Final Honour School was that 'its interest was romantic rather than scientific'. He added that 'as I consider that our Honour Schools are mainly valuable not so much for the information (useful or otherwise) which men acquire in the course of reading for them as for the mental habits they are calculated to form, therefore I ventured to resist the inclusion of Anthropology in its present stage of development among the subjects of the Final Honour School'. Acland does not seem to have borne a grievance. A letter to him from Spooner, a few years later begins with the words 'As you tell me that my letters sometimes give you help and pleasure'. But it was not until 1970 that Anthropology made its way into the list of subjects suitable for an Oxford Honours School.

good. It [?may] make some poor teachers less poor and save them from some mistakes but no teaching of the art will make a good teacher.

Spooner, on the institution of the Dip. Ed. as on so many other matters, is well in the middle of the road.

No account of Spooner's period as a Fellow of New College would be complete without some reference to his outdoor activities. In spite of his diminutive size and poor eyesight he was clearly quite energetic physically. Whenever it freezes he skates vigorously. In the vacations he goes for long walks in the Lake District and the Pennines. He rides, but not too energetically it seems; in May 1892 'I had a glorious ride on Saturday starting with Fisher [H. A. L. Fisher, who later succeeded him as Warden] and S. Hill but came home alone over Foxcombe, as I found they rode too hard for me – I never saw Oxford look more beautiful than it did from the top of Foxcombe: an old woman riding in a country cart made me stop and admire it'. In 1882, on his way to dine at Lambeth Palace, his horse fell with him in St James's Street. But he was still riding 'on Gerald's polo pony' in 1907, at the age of sixty-three. This may have been because of his failure at another method of transport; in July 1896 he is 'trying to learn to ride a bicycle in which for want of nerve I was not very successful'. Later in the year 'I took some bicycle lessons partly from a Professional partly from Mr Steadman but I make very slow progress and am doubtful if I shall ever learn'. Perhaps this episode gave rise to one of the best known apocryphal spoonerisms, 'the well-boiled icicle'. Though Spooner enjoyed riding, he did not approve of racing. In 1911, when he was Warden, he wrote to one of the Fellows about the 'grinds', a kind of College point-to-point, which had recently been held and

been attended by a good many of the Fellows including the
Dean.

> Perhaps this is better [he went on] than the indetermin-
> ate position into which they had drifted; but I am too
> old quite to like them being patronised by the Fellows.
> Disagreeable accompaniments are almost certain at
> times to crop up at race meetings and if Fellows are
> there it is rather hard to take cognisance of them.
> However, [he added characteristically] I honestly
> think this frank recognition is better than pretending
> they are not going on when you know they are.

When Spooner became Warden of New College he
became a public figure, and there are many descriptions of
him. But while he was still only a Fellow of the College not
much was published about him, and we have mainly to
rely on his own writings to discover his personality. However in May 1892 he wrote in his diary 'I was sorely put out
by a most unmannerly and in some respects untrue character of me in *The Echo*.' *The Echo* was a London daily newspaper, founded by Cassells in 1868, which expired in 1905;
at one period it was owned by Andrew Carnegie. Its issue
for May 4th 1892, under the headline 'Echo Portrait
Gallery', contains a 1,500 word article about Spooner
which, though it is not very good journalism, at least con-
veys something of the impression that Spooner then made
on his contemporaries. Spooner, the writer says, has written
no book with any title to greatness, nor is he a popular
lecturer; and he 'has been singularly unsuccessful in making
any decided impression upon his own college – misnamed
New – or in eradicating that abominable element of snobbery in which, unfortunately, this, the second college in the
'Varsity, has an unenviable reputation'. Yet 'he is certainly

one of the best known and most talked of men in Oxford'. The writer explains this on the grounds partly of his physical peculiarities and partly of his spoonerisms (the term is not used), of which he relates a few of the better-known apocryphal examples. The article continues

And yet, the hero of all these escapades is . . . a little clerical gentleman whose benevolent pink, clean-shaven face serves as a just index of a kindly and genial disposition, and whose only faults – even in the eyes of his pupils – consist of a certain absent-mindedness which makes him forget their names and appearance, and his special function as *censor morum*, which obliges him to impose penalties for non-attendance at Chapel and the neglect of college rules. At his residence Mr Spooner and his wife – a daughter of the late Bishop of Carlisle – make excellent hosts, although the master of the house, in characteristic fashion, has a trick of prowling round a guest and peering at him till he has made up his mind as to his identity. Indeed, now that Dr Sewell is over eighty years of age, the Spooners, with their musical evenings, are the main dispensers of hospitality in the College. At home our subject is certainly seen at his best, for he is too devoid of daring and of critical acumen ever to prove an efficient college tutor. [The writer considers that 'childish' is the proper epithet for Spooner's language on all occasions]: In the pulpit or at lecture, in his published commentary, or in his private notes, in his attacks on college offenders, or in his conversation with friends, his remarks are couched in the barest commonplaces. His hearers might be fourth-form boys, so anxious is he by constant reiteration to make clear the meaning of ideas whose only virtue lies in their infantile simplicity. [Yet the writer concludes that Spooner must have some share in] the success which has of late years crowned the efforts of New College in the 'Schools'.

More than once the omnipotent Balliol has had to bow the knee before it; and now that Balliol is seemingly on the wane there is no reason Mr Spooner's college should not catch up the falling mantle. In the honour that will then accrue to his college Mr Spooner will assuredly have his share.

Spooner commented ruefully in his diary that this article 'invented or retailed many silly stories, mostly fables, about me but it said some things that were true about a certain vein of childishness and inefficiency in my character and these things it was which riled me most'. Yet it is hardly likely that if this article told the whole truth about Spooner's character he would have been, eleven years later, unanimously elected Warden of his College. He was a much more considerable man than the writer of this rather impercipient article noticed.

For New College now, as *The Echo* suggests, had become a powerful and successful College, entirely transformed from the narrow and degraded institution it had been before the mid-Victorian reforms. It was now large and prosperous, and there were many distinguished men among its Fellows. It had gone through a period of stress and strain, as had the whole University, but it had finally emerged from these and assumed a stable and effective form, not much altered since except in its social composition (the 'snobbery' to which the article refers reflects what was then the almost totally public-school composition of its undergraduate body, perhaps the most important difference between Spooner's time and the present). The changed temper of Oxford at the end of the century is described in the opening sentences of the third chapter of his autobiography:

Fifty years have left Oxford in essentials the same; in external appearance, in many details and in several important particulars, greatly altered. Fifty years ago, it was still a close corporation, its teachers and students restricted in theory, though not in practice, to members of the Established Church; it is now not only a national but a cosmopolitan University. Its society was then predominantly but not exclusively celibate; married life among the teachers and Professors is now the rule and not the exception. Natural Science was then, as a branch of its studies, in its vigorous infancy; it is now in its less vigorous, but not less aggressive, maturity. Its numbers have increased by more than fifty per cent; its buildings, Collegiate and University, have been doubled. If in some particulars the beauty and dignity of the place appear to older observers to have been diminished, to many there seems to have been an added charm given to it by the blending of the new with the old which has taken place in the interval. The seething intellectual life, again, of fifty years ago, with its burning controversies, its fierce animosities and unsparing criticism, has been replaced by a more placable temper and a broader minded spirit; learning has certainly increased, ability, some think, has diminished; the desire to understand and to account for and explain has, to some extent, taken the place of the passionate love of truth which then prevailed, and has brought with it a more tolerant, if less self-sacrificing, spirit; there has been some loss, if much gain; and it is hard to weigh the one against the other.

This was the scene when the most important period of Spooner's life began.

A. C. Tait. From the portrait in the National Portrait Gallery by J. Saut, c. 1865.

Spooner as an undergraduate, c. 1865.

The Shirt. J. E. Sewell, caricature by
'Spy' (Leslie Ward), in New College
Senior Common Room, published in
Vanity Fair 1894.

The Spoo. Spooner, caricature by 'Spy' (Leslie Ward) in New College Senior Common Room, published in *Vanity Fair* 1898.

Alfred Robinson. From the
portrait in New College by
Sir Hubert von Herkomer.

E. C. Wickham. From the
portrait in New College
by Sir W. Richmond.

Hastings Rashdall. From the
portrait in New College by
Sir Oswald Birley.

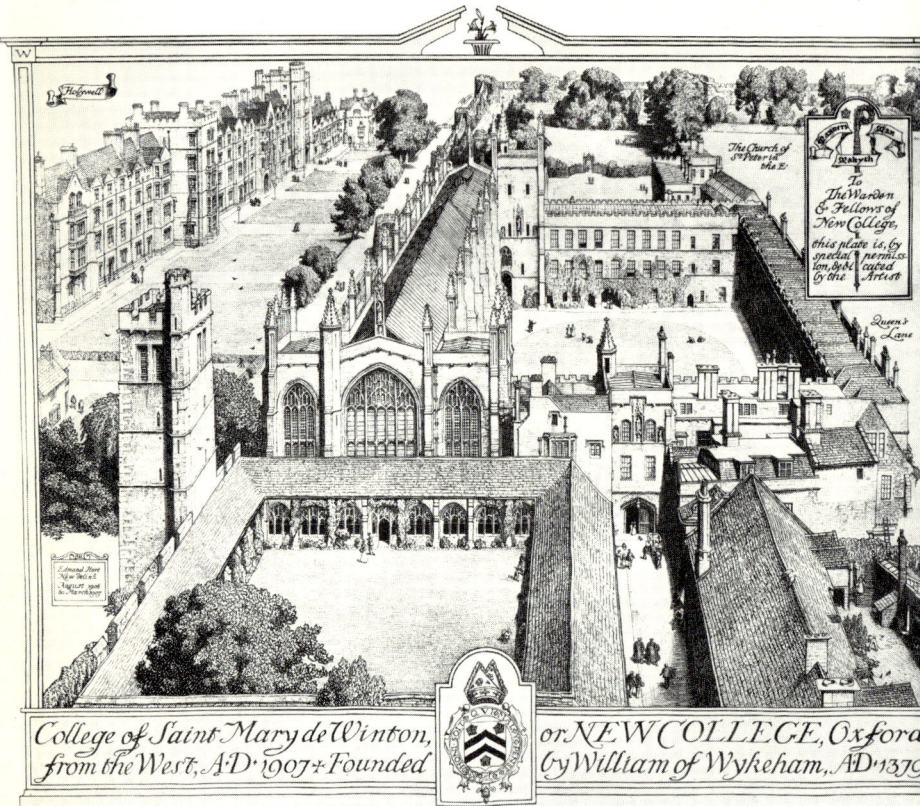

Within the engraving:

W

Holywell

The Church of
S.t Peter in
the E.

St Mary's Plate
Wakyth
To
The Warden
& Fellows of
New College,
this plate is, by
special permiss-
ion, dedi cated
by the Artist

Queen's
Lane

Edmund Hart
Nov.w Built A.d
August 1906
for Marchioness

College of Saint Mary de Winton,   or NEW COLLEGE, Oxford
from the West, A·D· 1907 ‡ Founded   by William of Wykeham, A·D· 1370

New College in 1907. From the engraving by E. H. New. The steep roof-ridge
in the bottom right-hand corner is the Warden's Barn. The complex of buildings
immediately above it is the Warden's Lodgings as altered by Caroë for Spooner.
Gilbert Scott's New Buildings are in the top left-hand corner.

The Warden's Garden, New College,
the Spooners' time.

The Warden of New College
and Mrs Spooner, c. 1920.

The Warden and Fellows of New College in 1921.
Back Row   H. H. Joachim, A. H. Smith, J. S. E. Townsend.
Standing   E. H. I. Schuster, E. H. Hayes, A. F. Walden,
            A. O. Prichard, J. S. Haldane, J. B. S. Haldane,
            H. H. Turner, L. G. Wickham-Legg.
Seated   H. L. Henderson, D. S. Margolionth,
            J. B. Moyle, W. A. Spooner, J. L. Myres,
            P. E. Matheson, H. W. B. Joseph.
On the Ground E. G. C. Poole, G. R. Y. Radcliffe.

CHAPTER V

Warden of New College

ON 9 MARCH 1903 Spooner wrote in his diary

I see there is a gap of more than six years since last I
wrote in my diary. They are years which have slipt
quietly away. One Fellow who has entered much into
my life came up just before the beginning of 1907 [sic]
Robert Rait of Aberdeen. He was elected a History
Exhibitioner in 1896 and become a Fellow before he
took his B.A. degree in January 1899. I only came to
know him well near the time he took his degree. Since
he became a fellow, he has become my chief friend
among the Junior Fellows, and we are very intimate.
Harold Butler, Arthur Butler's son, became first a
Scholar, then Classical Lecturer for a year and then a
tutorial Fellow. I have also come to know Professor
Turner, the Professor of Astronomy, well and our
clever young Professor of Physics, Townsend. – In
September 1901 Joseph broke down in health and had
to take a year's leave of absence, and I came and lived
and slept in College a good deal of the year, so as
partly to supply his place – Rashdall had also settled
down completely amongst us again and has become
our chief Philosophy teacher.* In this way there has

*Of the Fellows mentioned in this passage, Rait was co-author with Rashdall
(see page 82) of the standard history of New College. Harold Butler (1878–
1951) was a Fellow of New College from 1902–11, and afterwards Professor

97

gradually gathered round me a band of the younger fellows who are very loyal to me, men who I gradually felt would want me to be Warden should a vacancy occur. In 1902 I had been sub-warden and it was proposed at the October meeting that I should be reappointed for the ensuing year; but the proposal was objected to on various grounds and was dropped; and I nominated Moyle* Subwarden for 1903; and very fortunate the arrangement turned out as far as I was concerned. In November the old Warden being close on ninety-two gave notice to the Fellows of his intention to resign. He had been for more than two years in very failing health and had had lately great difficulty in even getting to Chapel or attending to any of his duties. I had to see him once or twice as to the date at which he wished his resignation to take effect and a very difficult matter it was to handle, as he wished to defer it to the following Michaelmas which would have made impossible any arrangements for the October term of 1903. But after he had announced his intention of resigning he got steadily, though not very rapidly weaker. I went to see him after my return from the Ordination at Peterborough† just before Christmas and found him then able to talk pretty well and he gave me some family reasons why he wished his resignation should not take effect till Michaelmas. On Christmas Day Frank and I took the old man a bunch of lilies of the valley as a birthday offering; but he was

---

of Latin at London University. H. H. Turner (1861–1930) was Savilian Professor of Astronomy. Sir John Townsend (1868–1957) was Wykeham Professor of Physics. H. W. B. Joseph (1867–1943) was the College's formidable philosophy tutor.

*J. B. Moyle (1872–1930), tutor in Law and for thirty years Bursar of the College.
†From 1902–1916 Spooner was Examining Chaplain to E. C. Glyn, Bishop of Peterborough.

when we went still in bed and not able to see us. However in the evening he came down and carved his turkey for Miss Fenwick and Miss Risley who came in to dine with him. This was his last considerable effort . . .

The New Year came in very quietly. We had a children's party to celebrate it on the 2nd. which went off with much spirit. The children, with Margaret Monck, acted a play, the *Snow Queen*, and did it with much spirit. We acted the same play again at the Workhouse a few days later and the people seemed to enjoy it very much. Directly this was over we went down and Cath with us to pay a visit to the Arthur Eastwoods in their new house Leigh Court near Taunton . . . We came back just in time for the Stated Meeting. At this our chief business was to receive the Warden's resignation which we did, and to pass a vote of recognition of what he had done for the College during his Wardenship. I helped Moyle to frame the words in which the vote was expressed. Besides we appointed a Committee to go into the sanitary conditions of the College and if possible to provide Baths.

Term began much as usual and I preached the first Sunday in Chapel . . . On Wednesday 28 January went up to the Workhouse School to be present at the Confirmation which the Bishop of Oxford himself took. When I got back to College Robert Sewell who was staying with his uncle told me that a great change had come over the Warden and that his doctor, Freeborn, did not think he could live the night. So after Chapel I went in to see him and read with him, as I had often done before in his previous illness, the commendatory prayer and some other prayers that seemed to me appropriate. The Warden seemed just to know me but was too feeble to speak. I kissed him and said goodbye and when I came down the next morning heard that he had passed away early in the morning without again recovering consciousness as far as they could tell. By a curious coincidence the Warden of Winchester, they had been elected in the same year, died on the evening of the same day. We had a meeting on Thursday to decide when and where the funeral should be and settled that the old man should be buried in the Cloisters on Tuesday, 3 February. Moyle who is Subwarden had to make all the arrangements, but I was put on the small Committee that was to help him to carry them out. I was also appointed along with Moyle, Courtney* and Joseph on a deputation which was to go to Winchester to attend the funeral of the Warden there. This took place on Monday 2 the day before our Warden's. At Winchester we had lunch with the Burges† but our time there was too short to enable us to see anything of the Masters. I saw rather more of the Provost of Eton and the Provost of King's.

Our funeral on Tuesday was very well arranged and stately. Rashdall, I and George‡ took the service between us but Margoliouth and Kirkby came in surplices so as to join in and the Bishop of Reading gave the blessing at the close. We clergy met the coffin at the door of the Ante Chapel but the Fellows, the Vice-Chancellor, the Scholars and Commoners gathered in the hall and making a great procession round the Quadrangle followed the Coffin into Chapel. The Heads of Colleges, the representatives of the Winchester Governing Body and the Bishops who were present had places inside the Chapel and so had the mourners and members of the family and the hono-

---

*W. L. Courtney (1850–1928). Philosopher. Fellow of New College for 52 years.

†H. M. Burge, Headmaster of Winchester 1901–1911, afterwards Bishop of Southwark and later of Oxford.

‡Hereford George (1837–1910), Senior Fellow, Author of *New College 1856–1906*.

rary fellows. Otherwise we had to keep it for present members of the College and the V.C. and his attendents . . . We went out of the Ante Chapel by the great W. door and the grave was in the N.E. angle of the Cloister . . . After tea at 5 o'clock there was a solemn conclave of Fellows – a most formidable gathering for me, at which we fixed Thursday 5 March at 12 o'clock as the day and hour for the election of a new Warden; but no one said anything.

There was just a month between this meeting and the time fixed for the election of a Warden, a whole half term and for the greater part of this time no one but Rait, who assured me I was likely to be elected, as there was no other candidate put forward, said anything. The Sewells slowly got out of the house, but we none of us went to see it, though I called on some of them. The Warden left a very small fortune only about £3000. He had given away a great deal of money to his relations in his lifetime . . . After about a fortnight George came and saw me one day and told me I might consider it settled I was to be Warden as no other candidate would be proposed; so I went after that happily but softly. I was put after this on a Committee which was to make arrangements for the election. We found the account of what was done when the last Warden was elected and settled that we would follow in the main the same procedure, tho' changes in the Statutes and the composition of the Fellows necessitated some changes. When our report came to be presented to the Fellows we were somewhat sharply divided on the question whether there should be anything in the nature of a religious ceremony at the Warden's installation. It was settled in the end that there should be; but there were strong dissentients . . .

The month before the day of the election 5 March slipped very quietly away. When the day of the election came – it was the same day on which Wykeham's first scholars took possession of the College – we had the Communion in Chapel at 8.30 . . . I was one of the Congregation. I gave one lecture at 10 but could not manage another at 11. The actual election was at 12, a good many fellows having come down the previous night. The election took place in the Chapel. It had been arranged the Saturday before that the Scrutineers should be George, Prichard and Professor Turner, George representing the ordinary Fellows, Prichard the Tutorial, Professor Turner the Professorial. The Statutes and Act of Elizabeth against corruption were first read by Margoliouth and we made the prescribed declaration. The scrutineers who sat at a table just in front of the Lectern voted first, while the rest of the Fellows retired to the Ante Chapel. Then Moyle called up the Fellows to vote one by one in order of seniority. When my turn came to vote, I did not go up, though some people thought I should have done so. There were I believe twenty-five fellows in all who voted and no vote was given except for me. The Scrutineers gave out the result and the fellows came and congratulated me. When it was all over I sent word home. The bells rang in the afternoon and again in the evening. As I walked about I received congratulations from many friends.

The 'word sent home' has survived and reads as follows:

> Dearest, I have been elected *nemine contradicente* – and did not vote for myself; but I do not know yet when I am to go to see the Visitor. I feel rather overwhelmed by the dignity just now; but I hope I shall get over it and rise to my position. Such a shaking of hands as there has been.
>
> Yours ever
> W. A. Spooner

The signature, from a husband of twenty-five years standing, is interesting.

The diary resumes the account of the almost Papal
ceremony of election and installation:

> It was agreed, as I have already recorded that there
> should be a short service for my installation at 4.30.
> At it we all wore our hoods. Moyle came and fetched
> me from my rooms and we met the other Fellows in
> Chequer. Then we made a procession through the
> Quadrangle to the Chapel where most of the Scholars
> and many undergraduates had assembled. When we
> arrived there Moyle, as Subwarden, conducted me to
> my stall and presented me after a little speech in which
> he stated my election had been formal in all respects
> with a copy of the Statutes, the College key and the
> College seal. Then the *Te Deum* was sung by the
> Choir, some prayers were read, a hymn was sung and
> I gave the blessing. After the Evening Service which
> followed we had another hymn and I again gave the
> Blessing.
>
> The younger Fellows all assembled in Hall to give
> me a welcome, as I had promised to dine; and George
> presided.* In the middle of dinner I had to make a
> speech to the undergraduates who received me very
> well; and in Common Room I made another speech
> to the Fellows – This, I think, was also approved . . .
>
> On Friday 13 March I went with Moyle to Lam-
> beth to be presented to the Archbishop of Canterbury,
> R. T. Davidson, who in the absence of a Bishop of
> Winchester, and as guardian of the spiritualities of the
> vacant See, acted though not without some hesitation
> as Visitor. It was a curious sensation to find him and
> Edith established at Lambeth, and to be received in the

*It is a peculiar New College custom that the Warden does not normally
preside in Hall.

Archbishop's room once more, with the Chaplain's room adjoining, so familiar to me.*

With this final act the long ceremony was completed and Spooner was definitively Warden of New College. That his election was unanimous is perhaps surprising; it is odd that there should have been no other candidate for this desirable post among the Fellows. That he should have been elected at all is much less surprising. He was in many ways the ideal candidate. The days of reform were over. The great reformers had gone; Robinson was dead, Wickham was Dean of Lincoln. Spooner was no reformer; he says of himself, in his time as Fellow, 'I have not nerve enough to propose the changes which would really make the place efficient'. But changes were not now needed. Consolidation was the order of the day. Spooner represented a middle position, not reactionary and not radical, prepared to hold the College steady on the course already set. He was generally liked, being quite without guile, but shrewd and with some steel behind the mild exterior. A. H. Smith, who became a Fellow in Spooner's time and was later Warden, says of him that he 'always appeared too innocent to be suspicious but had a singularly sharp insight into the motives of others'. Moreover he was an established Oxford 'character' already, as the *Echo* article quoted in the last chapter shows, and Colleges are not averse from seeing someone like that at their head.

As Spooner records in his diary, one of his first preoccupations as Warden was with his house. The Warden's Lodgings at New College are among the most beautiful in

*Archbishop Davidson was married to Edith Tait, Spooner's first cousin and the daughter of his god-father, Archbishop Tait, in whose time Spooner was often at Lambeth (he was for a time Examining Chaplain to Tait).

Oxford. The core of the house remains the rooms provided for the Warden when the College was founded in 1379. Once the Warden, at the Reformation, had escaped the obligations of celibacy it had been much expanded to accommodate his family. But in 1903 it was not in good condition. It had been neglected during the forty-three-year reign of Warden Sewell, who in his later years at least had refused to allow anything to be done to it. A. H. Smith, in his history of the College, describes how a young scholar in 1902 (evidently himself), 'summoned to the lodgings one October evening to read the declaration prescribed by the founder and to be admitted by the aged head of his college, could not but have the feeling as he passed through dimly lighted and silent rooms, that he had left the present and entered a strangely remote past.' Spooner himself writes 'My house gave me also a good deal of anxiety; it wants a good deal of actual repair as very little has been done to it in the late Warden's time and the offices and servants' quarters require to be reconstructed or often created entirely anew.' College tradition avers that Mrs Spooner, mindful of the glories of Rose Castle, thought that an Edwardian head of house should live on an episcopal scale, and certainly the reconstruction that followed created an almost princely mansion. There were sixteen bedrooms, and servants' quarters that included a larder, a game-larder, a scullery, a pantry, a servants' hall, a housekeeper's room, besides the huge fourteenth-century kitchen, with its stone-flagged floor and great coal-burning range, and various other annexes. A row of extra bedrooms was built on the roof to accommodate the eleven indoor servants, and there was another row on the second floor for the Spooner children (Sewell had been a bachelor). The reception rooms were on a grand scale, and there were stabling for four horses, a harness room and a big coach-house in the fourteenth-century Warden's Barn, which also contained quarters for the gardener and the groom. There was a walled garden with a Palladian summer-house and old fruit trees, to which Mrs Spooner added a mulberry, and a kitchen-garden in the Warden's Slype under the south wall of the College.

There was an initial difficulty about the architect. Moyle, the Subwarden, Spooner tells us,

> had already promised that Champneys* should complete the Quadrangle, so the actual repairs on that side had to be given to him. F and I were anxious that the reconstruction of the back part and of the offices should be given to Caroë.† This was ultimately agreed to by the College after we had ascertained that Champneys would acquiesce in, though he did not, I fear, like such an arrangement. I saw Champneys myself and conducted him over the House, so that I did not shirk my part of the disagreeable. The bringing this to a settlement occupied a good deal of my first week.

Next day he had a more agreeable experience; 'we spent a long day going thoroughly over the House with Caroë, who approved most of our suggestions and thinks he sees his way to making a nice house of it. My only fear is that he may do it at too great a cost'.

Spooner had in the past been unhappy about some of

---

*Basil Champneys (1842–1935) responsible for many Oxford buildings including the eastern half of the New Buildings at New College.

†W. D. Caroë (1857–1938) was also asked to reconstruct the Warden's Lodgings at Winchester. His grandiose plans for this were fortunately never carried out.

Champney's work in the College. In a letter to Rashdall on 21 September 1902 about some restoration work Champneys had been carrying out he wrote 'I am rather in despair about the spick and span appearance which the muniment tower has assumed; and the old glass alas! seems to have disappeared from the windows! I hope you and Rait will be more conservative of its contents than Champneys has been of its exterior'. And he is sharply critical of Champneys's contribution to the reconstruction of the Warden's Lodgings, in a long account of it which he wrote, which warmly praises Caroë's work. This praise might not perhaps be endorsed now. Although Caroë introduced some improvements, particularly to the staircase, his work has not been generally admired, and when my wife and I moved into the Lodgings in 1958 we undid most of what he and the Spooners had devised and returned the house to the size and something of the shape it had had before their time. Caroë's strangest invention was a rather bogus Long Gallery, facing north across a narrow lane and panelled in dark oak, which he formed out of various little rooms and which became the main sitting-room of the house; it looked like the 'Tudor Lounge' on a Great Western Railway express train. He introduced a number of fancy stone fireplaces with wriggling carving; 'the worm that dieth not' seemed to be his favourite device. But he certainly turned the house into something not far off a Bishop's Palace. Spooner contributed £3,000 of his own money towards the work on the Lodgings; it is not surprising that in 1904 he wrote in his diary 'Our finances are rather in a bad way; we have overspent ourselves, but I think with ordinary care and prudence it may all be put right'. Not long afterwards an aunt died and left him a considerable

sum of money. Of the furnishings of the Lodgings Sir Roy
Harrod has written 'The heavy mahogany and other
Victorian trappings that surrounded the shrimp-like figure
of Warden Spooner had a certain dignity, which matched
the true dignity and stability of Spooner's inner mind'.

In March 1904 Spooner wrote in his diary 'Saturday
March 5 was the anniversary of my election as Warden and
I felt all day a great thankfulness for the great and pleasant
position in which I have been placed; may I prove myself
not unworthy of it'. It had indeed been a notable year. He
had been asked to preach in Westminster Abbey. Dining
with the President of Trinity 'I was much impressed by the
magnitude of my office as I was sent in in front of Bryce,
an ex cabinet minister'. In April he had been asked to dine
with the Benchers of Lincoln's Inn, where he had been
pressed to 'take more wine than my abstemious habits and
weak digestion render desirable', and had had a long conversation with the Prince of Wales (later King George V).

He was very easy to get on with and told me a good
deal about his Colonial Tour* and the impression he
had got of the different colonies. New Zealand he
considered the most flourishing because of the almost
entire absence of poverty; and he thought that Mr
Seddon had probably the largest personal following of
any man in the Anglo-Saxon world. This he attributed
in part at any rate to his great memory for faces and
for the minute details of personal history. Australia he
considered had done itself much injury by the reckless
way in which they had cut down their wood. But in
Australia and New Zealand it was a pleasant feature to
see the way in which they kept the children to the

*The voyage of the Prince of Wales, then Duke of Cornwall and York, to
Australia, New Zealand and other countries had taken place in 1901.

front. The powers of organisation displayed by the
Colonials, particularly by the Australians, also impressed him. I liked the way in which he kept the
duchess to the front and made me understand that she
was associated in everything with him; it gave me a
pleasant impression of a thoroughly happy and
virtuous life.

He had dined at the Mansion House and had been received
Ad Portas at Winchester. He had been elected to the Club,
the most select of all Oxford's inner circles;

It consists of seven heads of Houses and five other
members and we dine together in term time four
times, i.e. every other week. We have a complete list
of members from its start. It was founded by a Cambridge man, Mr Bankes and started with ten members
in 1790 and my three predecessors have belonged to it.
Sir W. Anson* is our Secretary and preserves all our
traditions.

On Monday 29 February he had been presented at a Levée
by the Archbishop of Canterbury;

The ceremony seemed to me dull, but the dresses
magnificent and some of the wearers interesting. I had
lunch with them at Lambeth after the ceremony was
over and tea at the Athenaeum before coming back
home. My own dress is rather ludicrous, particularly
the gown with pudding sleeves and the three cornered
hat, which Nellie declared I should be stoned if I am
seen with in the streets. I did appear in the streets with
it and was not stoned, but the London populace seems
to take anything for granted on a levée day.

'A curious thing is official position' he wrote in June; 'it
seemed strange to me to be uplifted and put on a pedestal

*Sir W. Anson (1843–1914) Warden of All Souls and University Burgess.

through the whole of Commemoration'. Heads of Houses were then indeed the grandees of Oxford; the front entrance to Elliston & Cavell, the principal Oxford draper, could in those days only be used by the wives of Heads of Houses and of Canons of Christ Church, other customers having to use the side entrance.

But life was not all jollifications. At first he tried to combine the duties of tutor and Warden, but he soon found the routine work to be performed by the Warden more than he expected and gave up the tutoring. But he took on many other duties;

> I have been called on to preside at various public meetings – a meeting of the Army League at which Mr Lee spoke, and a meeting for Oxford House at which Lord Methuen* was the chief speaker. [One wonders if he may not have got these the wrong way round] Both meetings were in our Hall. Lord Methuen dined with me, and I thought him very charming, unaffected, straightforward, sensible, the model of what a soldier should be, though he is not, I should judge, a great general.

He also took on various more permanent responsibilities. He became a member of the City Education Committee, Chairman of the Trustees of the Warneford Mental Hospital, President of the Committee for the Acland Nursing Home, besides all his old commitments to Oxford House in Bethnal Green, to the Charity Organisation Society, to Lady Margaret Hall and the rest. But he seems to have enjoyed it all, 'very busy with correspondence, with the details of the house, and with my work on the Education Committee, but the variety of the work I have

*Field Marshal Lord Methuen (1845-1932).

to do I find an immense relief and a great pleasure to me'. However all this busy life put a stop to Spooner's literary production. His diary contains rather depressing allusions to his inability to get on with 'my book on the Apologists', which clearly never got written. 'I must try to organise my time better' he writes in January 1904. 'I spend a good many hours in work but to little purpose'. In 1906, 'I do not seem to have thought much or read much but had my time fully filled up; this is my great danger to let the details of life fill up every moment'.

The Spooners were also constantly entertaining and being entertained. Marconi and Elgar are among those whose presence in the Lodgings is recorded but undescribed. Lord Milner, a former Fellow of the College, is a frequent guest; in 1905 he 'looked desperately tired, as if he could never be rested again, but when he came to stay with us for his Honorary Degree in June 1906 he was greatly rested and had regained much of his old force and fire'. The same year there was a dinner in Milner's honour in London, which Spooner attended:

> Something like a vote of censure had been passed on Milner in the House of Commons* and this great gathering in his honour was a protest against it. Milner himself and Lord Curzon were the principal speakers and both spoke with great dignity and moderation. Mr Chamberlain who presided was not so happy. He flung a good deal of bitterness and contentiousness into his speech which was not the note we wanted. The dinner was attended by about 500 people, I met many friends there.

*The House of Commons passed a vote critical of Milner over the 'Chinese Slavery' question in March 1906.

In March 1904 Spooner 'dined with Rait to meet Lady Gregory and the Principal of Jesus. I found Lady G. clever and amusing, but she is fanatically Irish, devoted to the Scheme for saving the Erse language, and in her heart hostile to England. Fisher was at the party and it was very pleasant'. Of his own entertainments Spooner usually writes that they were a success; not invariably, however, for in October 1904 he entertained the Club for the first time; 'It was not a great success as Mackay our Lady Butler was not very clever with the wine'. But generally 'My attendance at the dinners of the Club is an ever growing pleasure to me and specially do I delight in the company of Mr Bellamy, the aged President of St John's'. He also continued to enjoy the Political Economy Club, and in 1903 for once describes a meeting of it in some detail;

> Dicey moved the question as to what causes had produced the reaction in favour of Protection and thought it was mainly due to the divisions among the Professors and the general trend of Legislation in a Socialistic direction. Charles Booth was there and declared himself in favour of a modified form of Chamberlain's doctrine, while Lord Hugh Cecil tried to show it was possible to oppose Chamberlain and yet support the Government. Fisher in the course of the debate made a good speech against Protection.

In 1905 an American lady, Mrs W. W. Campbell, whose husband was Director of the Lick Observatory in California and later President of the University of California, dined with the Spooners, and recorded in her diary her impressions of the evening:

> Dined at the Spooners. English women wore decolleté dresses. Catherine Spooner typical English cream and roses. Mrs S. splendid, highest type of refined clear-

headed able gentlewoman. Entered house by little Gothic pointed-arched door into a big hall with fireplace and stair-case of old oak, heavy, winding up past many landings. Drawing room narrow, crooked, piece of original stone buttress standing out, little old 2-light window up toward top of corner, Tudor ceiling. Bombay black-wood furniture, rugs, silver and brass little things. Warden's room over gate had fine oak mantel and panelling. Crests of Wardens. Portraits hung on panelling. Warden's study had a little place with slits in wall where he could look into Ante-Chapel and watch the boys. Low old stone doorway restored led to Mrs S's private sitting room, a retreat indeed, her own desk, books couch and little things in a quiet corner of the old pile. Up an old oak stairway narrow into a turret chamber with rafters of old oak where one of the daughters had her belongings, and a set of old oak furniture. Easy to lose one's way in the house. The Spooners had spent a lot restoring it besides what the College did. Dinner table was filled with things. Elaborate flower piece, two enormous silver mugs, tankards, I suppose, little clear glass pitchers of water, old silver, large salt cellars and pepper mills, silver dishes with the dessert around the flowers, candles and silver mugs. Menu tablets like easels at four corners. Two perfect maids in dark dresses with white vest fronts and collars and black ties, white caps. Thick brown soup, fish, partridges, sort of omelet, gelatine dessert with fruit in it, melon, apples, bananas, grapes. Coffee in drawing room. The English seem fond of fruit. Always have lots of it for lunch and dinner, often have very slight other dessert.

Spooner's social life was not confined to Oxford. There are frequent accounts of visits to London and elsewhere, but after one grand London dinner-party he writes 'I enjoyed this dinner, but was not sorry the next day to get back to the quiet and repose of Oxford', and after spending a Sunday at Cornbury Park he writes that he had met 'some rather nice but smart people . . . it was rather an offence to me that we only got to Church once'. He is inclined to be critical of people he describes as of 'the smart, empty headed sort', and after a visit to Eton he comments that the school is 'very much spoilt by thoughtless parents who come down in motor cars to see their boys and keep the place in a turmoil'. Spooner's opinion of Eton was not high. He tells us that Robinson, the Bursar of New College, was as a tutor at his best with

> the wayward, the careless, and those who had their intelligence still undeveloped. It was, I think, because he found in them so many latent possibilities waiting to be developed, that, like Professor Jowett, he seemed often more highly to value, and to be more successful in dealing with, his many Eton pupils than with those who came from schools which turned out more highly trained and finished scholars.

In October 1906 Spooner was elected to the Hebdomadal Council, the main governing body of the University. He took part regularly in its meetings; 'Being a member of Council gave me a good deal more work to do and I found it interesting; but I rather detest all kinds of Responsibility'. He declined the Vice-Chancellorship when his turn came. In University affairs he continued his middle-of-the-road stance;

> we have been debating in Congregation, [he writes in 1904] the question of requiring Greek in Responsions, and had a very exciting debate in which it was carried by two votes that Greek should not be compulsory for those who took Honours in Mathematics or

Science. This was a relaxation I was myself in favour of; as I am anxious to retain it for the mass of men but not in cases where people have really some other taste and knowledge and learn it merely to satisfy our University Examination. I have since been appointed a member of a Committee for drafting a Statute but at present have heard no more about it.

Next year

We had our great debate in Congregation on the question of compulsory Greek in Responsions. I was in favour of letting off the Honours men in Science and Mathematics, as I thought it would remove a burden which pressed heavily upon them and it might still be kept for the Pass men. However Anson spoke strongly against us on the ground we had not made sufficient provision for a literary alternative and Hadow on the strength of his experience in America and these two speeches carried the day and our statute was thrown out 200 to 166. I was not very sorry, as I think in any case there will have to be a reform in Responsions which is really what is most desired.

He was in the middle of the road, too, in public affairs. In March 1904 'Lyell got in for Dorsetshire wresting a seat from the Government; wrote to congratulate him as I am in favour of maintaining Free Trade and on the whole against Chinese labour in the Transvaal. Still I cannot say I should look with much favour on the Government going out'.

However much he may have disliked public and university responsibilities, he clearly enjoyed those that New College laid upon him. It has been said of him that at College meetings his presiding was almost imperceptible, but that he seemed to get his way, when he wanted it, without even having to ask for it. In his early days at any rate the College gave him very little trouble. In his first year as Warden New College went Head of the River;* 'this was pleasing to me, being associated with the beginning of my Wardenship, but I was still more pleased, because having a bump supper and a bonfire after it the men abstained from doing any mischief at all. They came and drew me for a speech and I made them one from my study window. This seemed to please them'. The college also won the Cricket Cup this year, and Spooner is reported to have said in his speech at the Bump Supper 'If I may use one of those transpositions of thought which are so unkindly attributed to me, may I say that our oarsmen have done it all off their own bat?' Next year again 'I had to make a speech to the men after Bump Supper which was very orderly and well-behaved'. Soon after he records that 'the College was certainly singularly free from noise or disturbance'. When, a little later, some men were caught climbing about on the roof of the Lodgings during a visit by the Archbishop of Canterbury (who slept through it all), they turned out not to be members of New College and were handed over to the Proctors.

But these halcyon days did not last. A. H. Smith, who came to New College as an undergraduate in 1902, in his history of the College gives a rather different picture of this period;

The freedom which undergraduates enjoyed in their social life and the costly amusements which their parental allowances permitted were shown particularly

*From 1884-1922 the New College boat was always in the first three, and in 1907 it rowed by invitation in the Olympic Games, defeating Norway and only being beaten in the final by Leander.

on Sunday nights when the College habitually gave itself up to extravagant festivity. On each Monday morning workmen arrived automatically to repair damage which had been done overnight, knowing well that their task would need to be repeated in the following week. These things were regarded as part of the general university life; but as time went on both the seniors and many of the juniors began to feel that they went too far and a greater measure of control was imposed.

Smith's last sentence is a veiled allusion to a particularly unpleasant series of incidents which occurred between 1909 and 1911. Accounts of what took place have been much overlaid by legend. There are stories of a Fellow of the College being crucified on the lawn with croquet-hoops, and of the destruction of a Fellow's life-time of research by marauding bands led by Duff Cooper.* Whatever the exact truth, it was clear that the College was becoming a rowdy and unpleasant place, unlike the peaceful and studious institution of Spooner's earlier days. This period falls into the seventeen-year gap (1907–1924) in Spooner's

*Duff Cooper's own account, in *Old Men Forget*, is different. Being involved in 'an unfortunate bonfire' and having burnt most of their own furniture, he and a friend

invaded the Senior Common Room and, having removed from it some of the more portable objects, ransacked the rooms of one of the junior Fellows which looked into the quadrangle where the fire was burning. It transpired afterwards that in the drawer of a small table which we burnt were some notes on which he had been working for three weeks. I was overcome by remorse and wrote at once an abject and sincere apology. The innocent and much wronged sufferer accepted my apology in the best possible spirit, but rumours spread round the University that I had destroyed the work of his lifetime, and that I had done it deliberately in some spirit of hate or revenge.

diaries, but two letters from him put the matter into some sort of perspective. The first of these was written on 19 May 1910 to the mother of an undergraduate, and seems to refer to the same incident as that in which Duff Cooper was involved; it reads as follows:

> I am sorry to say we have had to find serious fault with your son in a matter of College discipline. He with a number of other people was concerned in the lighting of a bonfire in College a week ago which led to the destruction of a considerable quantity of the property of the fellows, a lot of furniture and even some valuable papers having been destroyed. This is not the first time your son has taken part in offences of the kind and has had to be severely reprimanded about them.
>
> As however, he came forward and confessed his crime and told us afterwards frankly the part he had played in it and so made some small reparation for his misbehaviour, I felt myself not debarred from signing the certificate of character without which he cannot apply for a Commission, and I signed it after the matter of the damage done to the property of the Fellows had been cleared up, accordingly.
>
> I have had, however, to explain to him and I wish now to repeat to you, that I have to give a report of a much more confidential nature at the end of his time and what that report shall be will have to depend on what his conduct during the remainder of his career is, and I trust that it will be such as to enable me to give a thoroughly satisfactory account of it.

The second letter, dated 22 February 1911 and addressed to one of the Fellows, Harold Butler, refers to what seems to have been an even more serious affair:

> We are living rather uneasily under a condition of what the Dean calls 'martial law' i.e. most leaves are

refused and the men living in College are gated at 9 p.m. This has come about in the following way. One day last week a miscreant or miscreants painted and made a horrid mess of the archway and entrance to Joseph's staircase and made disagreeable and disparaging remarks on Joseph himself and so the Dean with my concurrence issued an edict that unless the culprit came forward by Sunday the College would be gated by Monday night for ten days. The culprits remained in obscurity and the College is now gated, so far much to the discomfort of us all but with no other disagreeable results. I think it is good to have put our foot down, but the process of keeping it down is rather exhausting.

The College certainly took a grave view of this incident. At the Stated General Meeting of the Warden and Fellows on 22 March of the same year it was agreed that 'in view of the discredit which had fallen on the College in consequence of recent disorders the Warden be asked to communicate to the Undergraduates that any Undergraduate found guilty of wilful damage to College property will be gravely punished'. A few days later Spooner sent a formal printed communication to every undergraduate:

Dear Sir,

In view of the riotous conduct which has lately disgraced the College, it is my duty to warn you as Warden that any undergraduate found guilty of wilful damage to College property will be most gravely punished.

Believe me,

Yours faithfully,

W. A. Spooner
Warden

Next month, on April 18th, Spooner wrote to an undergraduate who was obliged to go down because of ill-health

> I shall miss you in College because I think we want a steadying, sobering influence in College such as yours just now. Tho' I believe the College to be sound on the whole in greater things it is rather restless and rowdy and this has given it in some quarters a bad reputation which I hope the present generation will try to amend.

There is interesting evidence of the College's bad reputation at about this time in Frances Donaldson's *Life of Edward VIII*. In 1912, when the question of sending the Prince of Wales to Oxford was under consideration, Lord Derby, who had been consulted about the choice of College there, wrote to King George V 'There appear to be three in the running – Christ Church, New [sic] and Magdalen. New College I should not like as according to the Archbishop of York there is much trouble there'. By the time Lord Derby wrote this the troubles were in fact over. No doubt Spooner's stern admonition had contributed to their end. Dr Nathaniel Micklem, who was an undergraduate at about this time, thinks they were also partly cured because the Junior Common Room engineered some kind of internal revolution and managed to elect a very strong and responsible Steward; he records an impression that when he himself came into consultation with Spooner about this question he had the impression that the Warden knew all about everything that was going on in College.

This kind of mindless rowdiness was presumably the Edwardian equivalent of today's 'student troubles'; it is hard to say which of the two forms is the more distasteful. The Edwardian version is certainly very unattractive.

Perhaps the clue is to be found in Spooner's diary for March 1906. After reviewing recent arrangements for the Scholarship examination he comments 'It looks as if there were only just enough boys of any real merit to go round, and hardly that'. In those days, and indeed until much later, apart from a few boys on scholarships the College was filled up entirely with the sons of the well-to-do, with very little consideration of academic merit or desire to learn. It is true that New College was one of the earliest colleges to refuse to admit men to read for Pass Degrees and to confine its entry to those intending to read for Honours. But this hurdle was easily surmounted by a boy educated at one of the major public schools, and the College was manned by Wykehamists and Etonians, with a sprinkling of Harrovians and Rugbeians, mostly the sons of at least moderately wealthy parents, many of them regarding Oxford as a kind of finishing school and not seriously interested in work. They felt they were there as of right. In 1919, while Spooner was still Warden, a schoolboy of twelve was brought by his mother to visit New College, his father's college; he was introduced to the porter, who was informed that the boy would be coming up to New College in six years' time. This seemed natural and indeed inevitable to everyone concerned, including the schoolboy and the porter, and in due course it took place. Nothing like that would happen now. The boy when his time came would have to sit a serious competitive examination (as indeed this particular one did even then) and his father's former membership of the College would be of very little assistance to him. But all this was a long way off in Spooner's day.

Spooner's diary ceases, as has been said, in 1907. He made

regular notes on College meetings until March 1914 in another volume, but these refer almost entirely to routine College business. He also made full and detailed notes of his Progresses round the College estates, but these too are mainly routine in character. As examples:

> We went rather thoroughly over the Great Wood at Stanton. It seems in a very poor condition, scarcely a good tree to be found there. As the underwood and shooting rights are let to Mr Thomson, we recommend that nothing should be done there at present, only Skinner should be instructed when the underwood is being cut to see that as many young oaks are spared as possible and in some bald places a few trees might be planted. Nothing, however, considerable should be done except after taking skilled advice.

Or again

> Heyford. The ivy is getting rather worse than ever on the Church Tower and is now growing through the Belfry walls. I am sure it is endangering the security of the Tower. I cannot get this matter attended to tho' I have spoken about it for two years past. The Bursar takes no interest in it, as it is not his province. Mr Simpson whom I have asked to look at it makes no report upon it as he says he cannot examine it without a scaffold. Meanwhile the ivy though it has been a little cut goes on growing and endangering the stability of the fabric and if, as seems likely the tower falls down the College will have to subscribe to build it up again, when with a little care and thought the mischief might have been prevented. The village in my absence has had a bad epidemic of scarlatina among the children; the school has been shut up since the 14th May. Twelve out of thirteen cases or thirteen out of fourteen have been in cottages belonging to the College, almost all in the cottages on the right of the

street, as you go down the village. The drainage of
them, the people seemed to think was pretty good but
the village sewer runs down the opposite side of the
road and this is ventilated by open gratings without
any trap. . . . Mr Simpson should see to this the next
time he is here.

On one of these progresses Spooner made a remarkable
discovery. In July 1905 he visited Stanton St John, a village
near Oxford which has been in the College's possession
since the sixteenth century. The Manor Farm there had
been in the tenancy of a family named Harris for many
years; members of the family are mentioned in the parish
registers as early as 1667. Spooner in his Progress notes says
that the farm buildings were 'in a ruinous condition', and
that the farm-house was 'very dirty and wants a good
whitewashing throughout; some of the rooms are unusable
until they have been cleaned'. The Progress notes do not
refer to the most important event of his visit. In one of the
ruinous barns the Warden observed an oak chest, in use as
a corn-bin, the front of which was elaborately carved. He
bought it from William Harris, the farmer, for £50 (or at
least wrote off £50 worth of Harris's rent arrears to the
College). When the chest was brought back to New
College and cleaned up, the carving on it was identified by
Sir Charles Oman and others as a contemporary representa-
tion of the Battle of Courtrai, sometimes known as the
Battle of the Golden Spurs, fought between the French and
the Flemings on 11 July 1302. Mr Charles Ffoulkes, F.S.A.,
in a paper read to the Society of Antiquaries, says of the
Courtrai Chest that 'it is no exaggeration to state that it
ranks with the Bayeux Tapestry as a contemporary illustration of important historical events, and in some details it is

unique among the monuments of Europe'. What neither Ffoulkes nor anyone else has been able to explain is how this chest, carved presumably in Flanders in the early years of the fourteenth century, found its way to an Oxfordshire farm; all William Harris could tell the Warden was that it had been at his farm for more than sixty years. It remains in the Warden's Lodgings at New College.

The Warden's progresses continued unperturbed throughout the First World War, though on one of them in 1915 Spooner notes '22 men out of a population of 246 had gone from Stanton to the war'. In 1916 Ernest Barker* accompanied him as Outrider (a Fellow of the College is appointed to this office every year. His original duty was to protect the Warden from highwaymen as he went round the estates collecting the rents; now and in Spooner's time the office serves as a way of familiarising members of the College's Governing Body with the College's landed property). Barker in his recollections has a delightful picture of Warden Spooner on Progress:

> It was a lesson in history to accompany the Warden on his peregrination of those estates; it was also a lesson in all the arts of courtesy and charm to see how he had endeared himself to the tenants and their wives. The peregrination was well called a progress: it had almost a royal state. Church bells were rung to welcome the Warden's coming, 'vails' and 'regards' were distributed by the outrider according to ancient custom: here and there a manorial court was held in due style: here the tenants gave a lunch to the Warden (and such a lunch!) and there the Warden gave a lunch to the tenants. Even in the middle of the war the old ritual

*Professor Sir Ernest Barker (1874–1960) was a Fellow of New College from 1913–1920.

was preserved and the tradition of five centuries faithfully observed. But greater to me even than all the
ritual and the tradition (not but that I was moved by
it and deeply impressed by its values) was the bond of
affection between landlord and tenant which was knit
and maintained by the progress. In law, I knew, the
landlord was an invisible corporation, an 'artificial
person' styled by a legal name and living an unseen
life among the parchments of the archives and the
deeds of the bursary. In fact, or rather in feeling, I saw
that the landlord was the visible and actual Warden,
visibly and actually present on the estates and among
the tenants; remembering who each man was and
what his troubles were, and bringing the real presence
of a real person to establish a real bond of union.

But if the First World War made little change in the
Warden's Progress, its impact on the rest of the College's
life was heavy. The College was emptied of undergraduates. There was a tented hospital in the garden. Most
of the former rowdies were killed in France or in Flanders,
as were four of the Junior Fellows. Spooner wrote nothing
in his diary about the war, but we get occasional glimpses
of him at this time in other people's writings. His obituary
in the New College Record tells us that the number of
letters he wrote to men on service during the War was
astonishing. In one of these, dated 15 September 1918, he
wrote

We are just nearing the end of a long vacation and the
beginning of a new academical year, the fifth since the
war started. Even Lord Kitchener did not look forward to such a prolongation as that, and we in Oxford
certainly most of us thought that the war owing to its
great costliness must certainly end speedily. Now we
do not know what to think. We have just taken into

College a new batch of cadets to be trained into officers. They are to have a longer course than used to be the case, seven months instead of four; I hope you find them better prepared in consequence. I shall be very thankful to see many of you home again, though with terrible gaps. I think the end should be next summer and that our Gaude in 1919 may see us once again gathered together.*

Sir John Balfour recalls that when he was in a civilian prison in Ruhleben Spooner repeatedly wrote him charming letters. He did not restrict his letters to British old members. Baron Leopold von Plessen, a German member of the College, interned in Gibraltar and later in England, received from him 'long letters which I still possess. In his first letter to Gibraltar he wrote "hope deferred that makyth the heart sick" '.† Spooner kept his head remarkably well in a war when many others lost theirs. He was quite unaffected by the anti-German hysteria so much more

*The oft repeated story that Spooner said to one returning warrior 'Was it you or your brother who was killed in the War?', though it bears the mark of a typical Spoonerian confusion, is probably apocryphal since it is inconsistent with his habitual sensitive courtesy towards the young.

†Baron von Plessen tells one of the most delightful of Spooner stories:
Not knowing that gramophones were not allowed in College, I had my gramophone sent to me from Germany. When it arrived, my scout suggested that I explain the situation to the Warden and ask for his permission. Clad in my gown, I entered his study, slightly awestruck. I explained the situation at length – the expense incurred, my lack of knowledge of that particular regulation . . . All the time the little man looked at me through a magnifying glass which made his one eye very large At last he said:
'In consideration of the very special circumstances, I will allow you to keep your gramophone'.
'Thank you very much, Sir'.
'But you may nev-ah play it.'
(Privately printed reminiscences)

prevalent, particularly among non-combatants, in the First than in the Second World War. There was a number of German old members of the College in those days, Rhodes Scholars and others, and when the news of the death of any of them in battle occurred Spooner insisted on posting their names, with those of New College men killed on the Allied side, on the Chapel door. To objectors he would reply 'They too are members of the College, and they too have given their lives for their country'. When the war was over it was largely he who insisted on recording the names of the German old members who fell in the war on a tablet in New College Ante-Chapel.

An interesting example of his coolly detached attitude towards Germany is to be found in a letter he wrote to Milner on 20 December 1918:

> In all times of great triumph and excitement the nation must be in danger of losing its head for a time and there seems to be some danger of our doing this just now; personally I can think of few worse evils than to make Germany a tributary state to England and the Allies, and there is just a possibility, unless you and other sane men can prevent it, of our doing this through thoughtlessness and a sort of panic; such a condition of things, while it would be bad for Germany, would be infinitely worse for us and as a precedent exceedingly mischievous. I hear a good deal about Germany being taught a lesson that wars do not pay; but what if we, and others besides ourselves were to learn the lesson that they can be made to? The last state of such a nation would be worse than the first. Perhaps I exaggerate the danger.

Spooner went on to tell Milner of how the College was starting up again now that the war was over. 'Men are flooding back eagerly and very well and by January we shall have already made more than a start, by Easter we shall be half full, and by October our numbers will be as large as with a view to a succession they ought to be'. He thought there ought to be a memorial to commemorate 'the part the College has taken, headed by you and Fisher, in many ways and in many lands, in helping on the war'. Milner and Fisher, both Fellows of the College, were at this time respectively Secretary of State for War and President of the Board of Education in Lloyd George's Government. Fisher's appointment had delighted Spooner. On 9 December 1916 he wrote to him

It is a great surprise and a great pleasure that you are to be Minister of Education, and I congratulate you and the country too on your appointment. I know no one who can be more trusted to hold the balance true between the claims of Science and the Humanities in Education than you, and that will be no little part of your work in the immediate future. But it will be only a part, though not a small part of your work, and I shall be much interested to see what line you take up with respect to the W.E.A. I doubt whether our funds will allow us to support it in College to the full extent we have hitherto done and I think that in war time it is reasonable they should curtail their activities to some extent. In any case you will have in the office an experienced band of Wykehamical officials to support you and in Selby Bigg and Phipps you have two really good men. I was doubtful whether you would see your way to supporting Lloyd George on account of your known friendship with Asquith and his family; yet I think it was the patriotic line to take, and most of your friends will approve your action. The downfall of the late cabinet has been rather a trying shock; I imagine if they could have revealed more the late ministers could have made out a better case for themselves, and it is partly because they could reveal so little that *The Times* has had the advantage of them and been able to bring about their fall. Yet the fates and the ability of Germany have been much against them.

On 23 December Spooner wrote to Fisher again, saying

I cannot deny myself the pleasure of writing you a Christmas letter for many reasons, perhaps not least that I shall have the pleasure of addressing you as Right Honble. It is a proud position to have attained, and we in College are very proud to be able to count you among our Fellows. I am afraid it will be a position of much anxiety and great labour; but if you have in it, as I trust you will, a consciousness of good and useful work accomplished, well that is about the best reward a man can ask for.

The years after the war saw Spooner's apotheosis. He had become a legend in his lifetime. He seemed a survival from some remote and mythical past. An American who came up to New College in 1922 writes* 'I thought he had died in the eighteenth century'. He describes him as

The most feared man in New College, the man everyone scuttled from . . . a little aged albino with gleaming false teeth who blinked and smiled and ruled his roost . . . He used to send for me once every term or so and our colloquy was invariably the same:
    'Let me see, let me see. You're an Ameddican, an Ameddican. Aren't you?'
    'Yes, Sir'
    'An Ameddican . . . Did you ever know Felix Morley?' (Felix and his brother Christopher Morley

*T. S. Matthews. *Name and Address.*

had both been at New College: the Spoo was sure of them.)

'No, Sir.'

'Ameddica, Ameddica. *I* was in Ameddica once.'

'Yes, Sir?'

'Mmmmm-yes. I was in Paterson, New Jersey'.*

But attitudes towards him were generally more benevolent. There are numerous tales of his kindness to undergraduates. Sir Percy Loraine, a New College man who became High Commissioner in Cairo, met there another old member of the College, an Egyptian, who spoke affectionately of Spooner, recalling how the Warden had been most solicitous over blankets and warm clothing to protect the young Egyptian from the rigours of the English climate.† E. M. Hugh-Jones, who came up in 1921, had a serious accident in the hockey field. Spooner arranged for specialists and treatment at the Acland Home, which Hugh-Jones's family could not afford. Sir Roy Harrod recalls Spooner's comforting his mother when she was worried about her son's nervous condition, explaining that sensitive undergraduates often went through phases of melancholia. He was also known to deal kindly with a widespread New College complaint at this time, depression caused by the crushing nature of H. W. B. Joseph's dial-

---

*Spooner's visit to America is a little mysterious. In his diary for October 1896 he writes 'The Prince and Princess of Wales came to stay at Blenheim and a good many people went out to meet them. I was rather disappointed that we were not asked. I met the Duke of Marlborough soon afterwards at the giving of prizes at the Technical School but was not introduced to him. I should like to have been as I had met in America W. M. Vanderbilt, the duchess's grandfather (?)'. I have not been able to trace any other reference to Spooner's visit to the United States.

†See *Professional Diplomat* by Gordon Waterfield.

ectics. To some sufferers from this infliction Spooner would say 'You must not allow yourself to be depressed by Mr Joseph's criticisms; he is not always right'. To others who complained that they did not understand what Joseph was saying, he would reply 'Neither do I, but it doesn't matter'. On the other hand he could occasionally be somewhat disconcerting. An old member of the College was invited to stay the week-end, and at breakfast on the Sunday morning Spooner looked down the table and said 'Rolt, when are you going?' Mrs Spooner hastily intervened to say 'You know perfectly well, Archie, that Mr Rolt is staying until Monday'. 'Yes', said Spooner, 'but I wanted to see what he would say'. To my future father-in-law, Charles Hoare, then a not very well-behaved undergraduate at the College, Spooner said 'I hope, Mr Hoare, that your morals are not as tattered as your gown'.

Kind though he generally was to undergraduates, he frequently confused them, perhaps owing to his short sight. E. M. Hugh-Jones recalls being sent for and greeted with the words 'Good-morning, Mr Verschoyle, you have ploughed again in Divvers haven't you?' Hugh-Jones replied that he had in fact passed that examination, and that his name was Hugh-Jones. 'Yes', replied Spooner, 'very satisfactory. And now, Mr Hugh-Jones, what do you want to read? Do you want to read Greats?' On hearing that Hugh-Jones wanted to read Modern History Spooner replied 'Oh yes, I quite understand. You prefer to read and not to think don't you?', a reply which Hugh-Jones considers to have been a shrewd commentary not merely on himself but on the two Schools concerned. J. B. Murgatroyd, a contemporary of Hugh-Jones, recounts a similar experience. He was summoned and told that the Warden and his tutors were thoroughly dissatisfied with his continued misbehaviour and that he was to be rusticated. When Murgatroyd asked what his crime was, Spooner shuffled his papers, asked Murgatroyd his name, then stretched out his hand and said 'I, ah, am very pleased, um, to inform you that you have been awarded the Longstaffe Exhibition, and would like, um, to offer my congratulations'.

Sir Max Mallowan also suffered as an undergraduate from Spooner's confusions.

> I think I can fairly claim, [Sir Max has written], to be a living Spoonerism, for throughout my time he found it convenient to confuse me with a contemporary Wykehamist named Mallett, deliberately as I came to believe, and Mallett's crimes, all of a minor character, were imputed to me. 'Mr Mallett', he used to say, 'you have again been keeping late hours outside the College, and if you continue, I may have to gate you'. I sometimes wondered what he said to Mallett when his turn came. From my Public School training (at Lancing) I was well accustomed to a modicum of injustice and the Warden had a disarming charm of manner which made it appear boorish and rude to protest. Nevertheless at the third interview I began to do so, but he raised his hand in a deprecating manner and enjoined silence. I think he knew what he was doing and that the reproaches did me no harm.

All was not confusion, in any case. His letters to Rashdall and his other colleagues, both as Fellow and as Warden, show a clear-headed grasp of intricate College business. And many wise words are recorded. One old member recalls Spooner, in his sermon on the first Sunday of term, warning freshmen against 'the busy idleness of innumerable societies'. The effect of this injunction was, it seems, enforced by his distinct enunciation of each syllable, ending in a characteristically polite hiss of scorn. Imitations of Spooner's voice, mild, buttery, high-pitched, slightly lisping, are still current in New College, Sir Christopher Cox being a distinguished practitioner. Sir Christopher has written

> I hear him talking still with no difficulty. His voice was beautifully distinct and clear, perhaps a shade too sharp and lacking in resonance to be called bell-like, but getting on that way. He spoke very slowly, often with hesitations after or before words, and this lent excitement for the listener as to what he actually would say. You never knew what would come out, but whatever he said he did not change or amend.

Many Spooner anecdotes deriving from Sir Christopher Cox will be found later, in abbreviated form, in this book. It is much to be hoped that Sir Christopher will one day tape-record them in full, with appropriate intonations. The intonations, it is generally agreed, added great point to some of Spooner's deceptively simple-seeming but penetrating observations. Mrs Campbell of the Lick Observatory (see page 112) described Spooner's voice as having an 'unctuous accent', which she thought 'must render his -isms unbearably funny'. Another account of Spooner's voice is given by James Laver, who came up to New College in 1919 and who, in his book *Museum Piece*, describes a service in the Chapel and writes 'old Warden Spooner was part of the enchantment when, at the conclusion of the singing he rose in his stall (he was such a little man that standing made no difference to his apparent height) and in a thin, quavering voice, pronounced the blessing'.

Everyone at this time concurred in believing that

Spooner, by some kind of intuition, knew everything that was going on in the College. Sir Max Mallowan thought this was because he had a good Intelligence Service. Sir Maurice Bowra, who came to New College as an undergraduate in 1919, had a different explanation. 'Spooner', he writes in his *Memories*, 'was a kind of Lob, with a touch of fairy-blood. He moved in his own world and had an elfin clairvoyance into our characters and doings. I cannot think how he did it. He had no spies, and he was much too blind to see what we did, but none the less he knew'. The best known example of his clairvoyance had occurred many years earlier. In 1904 an undergraduate in his last year was summoned to see Spooner:

'Ah', began the Warden, 'Quite so. I think when you came up to Oxford you had every intention of taking Holy Orders?'

The undergraduate murmured something unintelligible and waited.

'And I am afraid that you have quite abandoned the idea?'

'Oh rather, yes, quite, Mr Warden, quite given it up'.

'And what do you propose to do?'

'Well, I want to be a schoolmaster, I've done a little at odd times and like it awfully, so I think of going in for it permanently'.

'Oh yes, a schoolmaster, really. Well, Mr Woolley, I have decided that you shall be an archaeologist'.*

And so began the most distinguished archaeological career of the twentieth century, leading to the great excavations at Ur of the Chaldees. Sir Leonard Woolley comments 'I was not quite sure what an archaeologist was, but

*See Sir Leonard Woolley's *Dead Towns and Living Men* (dedicated to Spooner).

there was no gainsaying Warden Spooner, so I became one, and I have never regretted it. Work in the Ashmolean Museum, on the Roman Wall, in Egypt, in Italy and at Carchemish filled me with gratitude to the pastor and master who had thus "decided" on the course I was to follow'.

There are many tributes to Spooner in his last phase. Sir Julian Huxley, in a BBC broadcast, said of him that 'Though he published very little, he was a good scholar and a good teacher. He was an excellent administrator, with the rare gift of making people feel that he was deeply involved in their own particular affairs. He worked very hard without any thought of self, and gave the impression of possessing that rare quality which I can only describe as saintliness'. Sir Roy Harrod has written 'In my life-long career at Oxford I have known many very distinguished heads of Oxford and Cambridge colleges, such as J. J. Thompson, Tommy Strong, H. A. L. Fisher and Maurice Bowra. In my opinion Spooner, having regard to his scholarship, devotion to duty, and wisdom, overtops them all'. And Sir Ernest Barker, who in his lifetime was a member of five Oxford colleges and one Cambridge college, writes in his memoirs that Spooner was 'the shrewdest and wisest and kindest of all the heads of colleges whom I ever served'. Barker describes New College as 'a happy ship, and the happiness came from the captain', and he adds 'his genius was a deep personal interest in the persons and personalities of all the members of the College; and the genius brought him success, as it also brought him affection'.

But in this genius there was an odd, minor flaw, and curiously enough it was this flaw that brought him lasting fame.

CHAPTER VI

Spoonerisms

Spoonerism [f. the name of the Rev. W. A. Spooner (1844–
——).] An accidental transposition of the initial sounds, or
other parts, of two or more words.

Known in colloquial use in Oxford from about 1885.

1900 *Globe* 5. February. To one unacquainted with technical terms it sounds as if the speaker were guilty of a
spoonerism.

O.E.D. (1919 Edition)

To a delinquent undergraduate:
'You have tasted a whole worm. You have hissed
my mystery lectures. You were fighting a liar in the
quadrangle. You will leave by the town drain.'

Of a cat falling from a window:
'It popped on its little drawers.'

In a sermon in New College Chapel:
'Which of us has not felt in his heart a half-
warmed fish?'

At an optician:
'Have you a signifying glass?'
'?'
'A *signifying* glass?'
'Er, I don't think we stock them.'
'Oh well, it doesn't magnify.'

Did he ever actually perpetrate one? All the above, and the many other similar ones, are obviously apocryphal, invented by undergraduate wits (or according to one account, by W. W. Merry, then Rector of Lincoln College) and fathered upon him. But clearly he would not have been chosen as the putative father for such inventions unless he had at some time engendered something similar. It is reported that at his last Gaude he made an impeccable and charming speech and then, at the end, said 'And now I suppose you will expect me to say one of *those things*', and sat down. Professor Charles Manning, at that time a Fellow of the College, recalls that in this speech Spooner said that he would not describe his feelings – 'I would not if I could and I could not if I would'. Professor Manning comments that at this point, 'there was an almost audible sigh, not from him, as if he had succeeded in the walk along a tight rope'. There are only two references to spoonerisms in the diaries. In an entry for 9 May 1904 he records that 'I went up to London and stayed with John Murray for a meeting of the Royal Literary Fund . . . I sat at dinner between Mr Craigie and Sir G. Newnes* . . . Sir G. Newnes . . . invited me to his house, a competent man of business. He seemed to think he owed me some gratitude for the many "Spoonerisms" which I suppose have appeared in *Tit Bits*.' At the very end of his diary, in October 1924, he mentions sitting next to an American lady at a 'Classical Concert': she

accosted me by asking whether I was Dr Spooner. I said I was and she replied I was the best known name in America except Mr Hudson Shaw who had organised Lectures there. She professed to have found it a great pleasure to have sat by me and talked to me; and

*Sir George Newnes (1851–1910) the newspaper magnate.

I think it was; for to have known a celebrity, even the author of 'Spoonerisms' means a good deal, tho' I explained to her that I was better known for my defects than for any merits.

In a letter he wrote to his wife during a visit to South Africa in 1912 he says 'The Johannesburg paper had an article on my visit to Johannesburg, but of course they thought me most famous for my Spoonerisms, so I was not greatly puffed up'. New College oral tradition is that he admitted giving out the hymn in Chapel as 'Kinquering Kongs' but denied all the rest. I asked Rosemary Spooner about this, and she replied 'I never understood how kinquering kongs originated because we never had the hymns given out in Chapel – they were just on the printed sheets'. She added that 'The question of Spoonerisms was never mentioned in the family!' and that she thought the only time her father ever referred to them publicly was the veiled allusion in the Gaude speech mentioned above.

There is in fact very little doubt that Spooner did on occasion fall into metaphasis, the technical term for this transposition of sounds (*Punch* once referred to him as 'Oxford's great metaphasiarch'). The trouble is that the authentic metaphases are usually less neat and pointed than the apocryphal ones of the type quoted at the head of this chapter. Professor Henry Price, a witness of truth if ever there was one, heard him say 'In a dark, glassly', and there is corroboration of this one, if corroboration were needed, from several sources. Sir Charles Oman reports hearing him, at a meeting of the Political Economy Club, refer repeatedly to 'Dr Childe's friend' as 'Dr Friend's child', and Dr Micklem's brother was told that the story of the Flood was 'barrowed from Bobylon'. David Butler says that

when Spooner officiated at his parents' wedding he spoke
of them as being 'loifully jawned in holy matrimony'.
There are first-hand accounts of him telling a group of
undergraduates 'I am very sure of one thing, gentlemen.
You will find as you grow older that the weight of rages
will press harder and harder upon the employer' (one of the
undergraduates commented 'Well, I've been up for four
years, and never heard the Spoo make a spoonerism before,
and now he makes a damned rotten one at the last minute').
And there seems to be little reason to question the often
repeated account of Spooner observing in a lecture 'Gentlemen, on this point Aristotle was mished'. ('Mished' for
'misled' became for many subsequent years a common New
College usage). Sir Julian Huxley relates that

> after a discussion about our expedition to Spitsbergen,
> in which I had stressed its easy accessibility in spite of
> its high latitude, he remarked to his wife 'My dear,
> Mr Huxley assures me it is no further from the north
> coast of Spitsbergen to the North Pole than it is from
> Land's End to John of Gaunt'. Mrs Spooner, a large
> and majestic woman, fixed me with a stony look: I
> didn't even smile.

There is another first-hand account, by Reginald Jennings,
of Mrs Spooner's stern attitude to spoonerisms:

> *W.A.S.* 'I'm sorry to have to leave you, but I have
> to dress for Chapel before Hall'.
> *Mrs Spooner:* 'Archie!'
> *W.A.S.* 'Oh! Have I said another of those things
> again?'

It is doubtless because there were occasional lapses of this
kind that the apocryphal inventions were fathered upon

him. But as Sir Ernest Barker suggests, he was 'seldom guilty of metaphasis, or transposition of sounds. What he transposed was ideas'. Sir Ernest himself, in the course of one conversation, heard Spooner say Athenaeus when he meant Aulus Gellius, and Grotius when he meant Grocyn. And there is the well-known story of the sermon which referred throughout to Aristotle, in rather surprising contexts, at the end of which, after a brief pause, Spooner is supposed to have said 'In the sermon I have just preached, whenever I said Aristotle, I meant St Paul'. But the matter is generally more complex than this. There is the well-authenticated story of Spooner walking with a friend in North Oxford and meeting a lady dressed in black, to whom he lifted his hat. When she had passed 'Poor soul', he said, 'very sad; her late husband, you know, a very sad death – eaten by missionaries – poor soul!' Then there is the undoubtedly authentic story of Reggie Coupland being greeted by the Warden, as he emerged from Chapel, with the complaint 'Mr Coupland, you read the lesson very badly'. 'But, Sir, I didn't read the lesson', replied Coupland. 'Ah, I thought you didn't' said Spooner. This could I suppose conceivably fall into the class of those Spooner remarks, of which the Casson story is the most famous, where one is not quite certain that he was not doing it deliberately, as what Sir Maurice Bowra calls 'an embarrassment game'. The Casson story, readers perhaps scarcely need reminding, is that Spooner met Stanley Casson, a rather brash young archaeologist in those days, in the Front Quadrangle, and said to him 'Do come to dinner tonight, to meet our new Fellow, Casson'. Casson replied 'But Warden, I *am* Casson', to which Spooner replied 'Never mind, come all the same'. Nothing of this kind explains the

story told by R. F. Horton, in his autobiography, of hearing
Spooner say at a meeting of the Charity Organisation
Society, 'The case of this boy came before us, you remember, *next* week'. But some of his apparent confusions
were full of point. For instance, when told that a secret
passage ran from Campion Hall (the Jesuit house in Oxford)
to Pusey House (the Anglo-Catholic centre) he replied:
'That may be, but it runs the other way'. And it is reliably
recorded that when there was a discussion about admitting
to New College Krishnamurti, the Indian mystic, said by
Mrs Annie Besant to be an incarnation of Jesus, Spooner
said 'Next we come to the name of Mr Krishnamurti. I
understand that Mr Krishnamurti is supposed to be an
incarnation of Our Lord, so of course we can't have him at
New College'.

Two rather baffling stories are recounted by Sir Roy
Harrod. As an undergraduate at New College, he was asked
to tea with the Warden. This was in 1917, when drinking
port was for some odd reason held to be unpatriotic.
'People warned me', said Spooner, 'that if I gave up port I
should be less amusing, but I do not find myself any less
amusing than I was before'. Then there was Sir Roy's last
encounter with Spooner, in Peckwater Quadrangle at
Christ Church.

> I ran so as to overtake him. I said I was sorry we did
> not see him more often in Christ Church. 'Well', he
> said 'I am hesitant to go there more often, because I
> am afraid of interrupting them at their prayers'. Of
> course he knew perfectly well that Christ Church was
> not a College especially addicted to prayer, and even
> if it was he certainly would not expect to find people
> kneeling about in the quadrangle saying prayers.

Then there is a rather strange story related by Sir Christopher Cox, who heard it from A. H. Smith. At a College meeting there was an interminable discussion of the question whether there should be one gate or two gates at the Non-Licet entrance into New College from Queen's Lane. Spooner concluded it by saying 'My own view, for what it is worth, is that two gates – are – quite enough'. This could, of course, have been deliberate, but Sir Christopher Cox has some other first-hand stories of Spoonerian confusion for which no explanation other than genuine incoherence is conceivable. On one occasion, Spooner, on being asked by Sir Christopher about a car accident in which Mrs Spooner's finger was injured, replied 'they mended it on again afterwards – but she lost it – *permanently*' (long pause) 'for the time'. Then he said to a former member of the College who was lunching with him 'I hear you are serving in Liberia', and on being told that it was in fact Nigeria, replied 'How far are you in Nigeria?' In both these two incidents there seems to be a certain confusion in Spooner's mind between time and space.

Some of his spoonerisms were physical rather than verbal. The most famous is described by A. J. Toynbee:

> The acted spoonerism was witnessed by my mother's old friend Eleanor Jourdain. At a dinner party in Oxford, she saw Dr Spooner upset a salt-cellar and then reach for a decanter of claret. He then poured claret on the salt, drop by drop, till he had produced the little purple mound which would have been the end-product if he had spilled claret on the table-cloth and had then cast a heap of salt on the pool to absorb it.

His diaries and his other writings contain few or no spoonerisms. He makes the kind of occasional slip of the pen that we all make, writing 'coast' when the context requires 'ghost', writing 'frillitaries' for 'fritillaries', inventing an interesting new Italian painter called Tintarello. One of these slips has a comic effect. Reflecting on his fiftieth birthday in his diary for 22 July 1894 he writes 'My wife has been in many ways a singularly peaceful and happy [?"one" omitted] but more limited than I had once hoped'. In his book on Bishop Butler there is a passage which has the mysterious, baffling quality of his conversation with Coupland about reading the lesson. He describes how Butler fitted up his house in Hampstead with some magnificence and taste, and to this he appends the following footnote: 'Some of the stained glass with which the staircase was adorned was subsequently presented to Oriel College, and is still in the possession of that society; but of the details of the gift, and even of the name of the donor, no record seems to have been preserved'. The more one studies this footnote, particularly the last sentence, the more perplexing it becomes. Something of the same quality appears in a passage in the Introduction to his *Histories of Tacitus*, where he writes that 'to forget is not equally easy with being silent'. There are legends about mysterious Spoonerian letters, but none of the letters have been preserved; the best known of these vanished letters is one urging a friend to come and see him the next morning on an urgent matter (not identified) to which Spooner added a postscript that since the urgent matter was now settled there was no need for the friend to come. Sir Julian Huxley mentions a letter which Spooner had signed 'yours very poorly'. He then drew a line through 'poorly', leaving it perfectly legible, and replaced it with 'truly'. In another letter, written to the relative of some one just recovered from a serious illness, he

wrote 'I am so glad to hear that you are at last relieved of
your terrible burden of debt'; 'debt' was similarly crossed
out and replaced by 'anxiety'.

Sir Julian suggests that Spooner must have had something wrong with some of the association centres in his
brain, which led to his writing or saying the wrong word,
or in some way making the wrong association, but that this
did not prevent him being very efficient in the varied
intricacies of college business. The medical aspects of
Spooner's confusions are examined in a paper entitled *Dr
Spooner and his Dysgraphia* by Dr J. M. Potter, published in
the *Proceedings of the Royal Society of Medicine* and originally
delivered as a Presidential Address to the Section of Neuro-
logy of the Society at Oxford on 26 March 1976. I have Dr
Potter's permission to quote here from the concluding
passage of this very interesting paper:

> In conclusion therefore, I should like to make three
> tentative suggestions. First, that Spooner's form of
> cerebral dysfunction may represent an intermediate
> state between the slips of the tongue, pen and action –
> the lapses, dyspraxias or absentmindedness that are
> Freud's 'parapraxes' of everyday life – and the gross
> dysphasias and dyspraxias of overt disease and damage,
> often with predictably demonstrable pathological
> lesions of certain areas of the brain. The everyday
> lapses are the concern of linguists and psychologists;
> they are not yet sufficiently approachable by the sort
> of scientific precision demanded by the physiologist;
> there is no known pathology, and they are not medi-
> cal. There is thus a substantial disciplinary gap between
> them and the florid dyspraxias of language and action
> familiar clinically to neurologists and neurosurgeons
> and, later as their causative lesions, to neuropatho-
> logists.

My second tentative suggestion is that a developmental disorder is the most likely explanation of Spooner's striking example of an individual variation. We have no means of knowing whether or not he suffered some self-limiting disease, possibly one acquired during childhood, but this seems less likely as a cause of brain damage so subtle as to be manifested only by such sporadic lapses.

Third, I should like to entertain the possibility that there may be others with Spooner's degree of disability who, not being in his intellectually exposed position, pass unremarked. Their progress at school would not necessarily be retarded, so one would need to seek them out with even more diligence than is required to discover dyslexic children who were, after all, largely unrecognised until comparatively recently. Though now actively sought and increasingly recognised, even the dyslexic child is perhaps not yet entirely understood. Moreover, an organic basis for the condition is not conceded by 'nurturists' who appear to believe that environmental influences can somehow act independently of the organ which alone can process them, the genetically developed brain. It seems possible to me that the Spooner trouble might be regarded as an essentially motor member of that family of developmental disorders which has developmental dyslexia as its outstanding example.

Finally, Dr Potter hints at the possibility that Spooner's albinism could conceivably have some connection with his lapses into confusion. That there was some kind of physical cause for these lapses seems likely enough, though there certainly seem to have been occasions (the Casson story, the Coupland story and perhaps the story of the two gates) where Spooner was able deliberately to exploit, or even create, a confusion to get out of a difficulty. Whatever the explanation, it is certainly ironical that the man who received, and merited, the tributes from eminent men quoted at the end of the last chapter should now be chiefly remembered for the trivial absurdities, most of them apocryphal, recorded in this chapter. But such is the fate of academic persons. They may possess great influence in their lifetime. But unless they publish work of lasting value their reputation dies with them, or survives only as long as their pupils. A parallel case is that of F. F. Urquhart. Born eleven years after Spooner, for many years Dean of Balliol, known to everyone as Sligger, his influence extended all through the University. But he published nothing, and had not even a quirk like spoonerism to keep his memory alive. Whether Spooner would prefer this kind of survival to total oblivion is perhaps doubtful. He was quite sensitive to references to the subject. Sir Maurice Bowra recalls how when, at a New College Gaude, a Judge of the High Court made some ponderous joke about it, 'Spooner replied sharply, comparing himself with Homer and Shakespeare to whom works not their own were attributed and arguing, that if the same were done to him, "I err in very good company".'

CHAPTER VII

Spooner's Characters

SPOONER SEEMS TO have enjoyed writing descriptions, character studies, of his friends and acquaintances. There are a large number of these in *Fifty Years in an Oxford College*, and others, less formal, in his diaries. Many of the people described are no longer of much interest; some of them are still remembered, at least in academic or ecclesiastical circles.

One of the characters to which he devotes much attention is his own. His autobiography is strikingly impersonal, but in his diary he often comments incisively and quite critically on his own qualities, feelings and shortcomings. In August 1881 he writes

> I cannot quite attain a consistent system of philosophy but sometimes seem to myself to be coming near it . . .
> At present my publishing ventures have not been much of a success. The SPCK would not accept my political economy and I can get no pay for my work on the *Ethics*. I hope some day to make up by diligence for my want of cleverness. Every now and then a great yearning to be clever and famous comes over me but I know in my heart that I have not got it in me. My mind even in sermon writing moves slowly and thoughts do not readily come.

Later that year he meets the Bishop of London and writes in his diary 'I am in hope that some day he may appoint me Whitehall preacher, an office which I should greatly like (partly as a means of getting known) but I am afraid he has already promised it to someone else'. When he got back to Oxford 'I have found more satisfaction in my Lectures than I generally do, but each year it becomes to me more difficult to concentrate my attention on any subject'. Summing up at the end of the year he writes 'I am not yet very good as a Lecturer. Perhaps I do not work hard enough . . . In knowledge I fear I have not added much to my information'. Early next year, staying with his mother and sister after a happy visit to Rose Castle, he writes 'I find it hard to be cheerful here and am apt to be peevish and morose'. Next year when his son Billy is born he reflects 'I trust that he may grow up into a good and useful man, but knowing my own failings and sins I feel the responsibility of a child very much. One can only pray "deliver him from evil" '. In September that year he wrote 'Began some more regular notes on Tacitus' *Histories* and enjoyed the work. Yet I rather feel of myself unstable as water thou shalt not excel. In matters of principle and diligence alike I have much instability'. At the end of the same month he is writing

I have got uncommonly little done this week. Alas! Alas! If I could only learn Carlyle's lesson of *work*, it would be something. My powers are not great, but I fear I do not do my utmost with them. Correspondence, trifles, all kinds of things interfere with work and make up life. It will be twenty years when I go up to-morrow since I first went to Oxford! What a long slice of life to have spent there – term by term – more than half mine. None of it spent quite idly and yet nothing, I fear, wholly mastered, made my own. That is my weakness – I have not *much* assimilative power and sadly lack originality. Yet what we have *not* depends upon God as well as what we have and it is no good any way to repine.

A day or two later

It is twenty years since I first came up October 1862 – What a large slice of life. I have gained in some ways, but have, I fear, reached the end of my tether and shall never be more than I am – a moderately useful man. There have been troubles in these twenty years ... yet they have been in a way happy and prosperous too. Sometimes, I fear, I have shirked responsibilities yet I try not to. I cannot make myself a good lecturer or a learned man do what I will; yet I have some influence and what I have I try hard to make for good. I intend to try and work better and lose less time. May I have strength for this.

But at the end of the year he is writing again

This year I have had more satisfaction in my work in College, but have hardly laboured at it as hard as I ought. In the Vacations the time somehow slips away and I get little done; then my lectures are not ready for term. I feel as if I had reached the end of my tether, [he repeats this odd phrase] shall never, I fear, be more than I am.

As already recorded, in his comments on the article in *The Echo* in May 1892 he alluded to 'a certain vein of childishness and inefficiency in my character'.

On 22 July 1894, his fiftieth birthday, he wrote in his diary

Most of the exuberant pleasure in life behind me now and have to look forward to going down the hill. My wife [sic] has been in many ways a singularly peaceful and happy [?'one' omitted] but more limited than I had once hoped. By 50 everyone must have taken pretty well the measure of his own powers and mine have certainly not expanded as once I hoped they might have done. On all sides I find there are limits and limits rather easily reached. I am, I hope, to some extent a useful kind of drudge but not a ruler of men. I cannot influence or impress people, as once I hoped to do: now my chance of doing so has, I fear, passed.

In 1896 he writes 'Willie Donne appointed Chaplain to the Queen – how others pass me now in the race of life. I fear I must be content to do quite small things. May I have grace to do them faithfully and without repining and to the best of my power'. At the end of the year he writes 'I read a good deal of Butler but did not make much progress with my book. I always find it so hard to screw myself up to write at all. Thoughts do not crowd in on me nor have I a constructive imagination'.

It is interesting that these rather unhappy notes cease to sound when Spooner becomes Warden, though they re-appear after his resignation. While he is Warden he complains once or twice of his inability to concentrate or to use his time fruitfully, but there are also occasional hints of an unusual complacency. Describing the Gaude in 1905 he writes 'people liked my speech, which was I think a hit'. But he never became conceited.

Spooner's characterisations of other people were of course more formal and continuous than that devoted to himself. In Chapter III of his autobiography there is a long section devoted to the University preachers of his younger days, when the University pulpit was still 'a great feature and power in Oxford'. The doyen of these was Pusey, who in Spooner's time was the undisputed leader of the Oxford Movement, and who had once been suspended for two years from preaching to the University because of a sermon suspected of papistical leanings. Sara Coleridge says of his preaching that 'he is as still as a statue all the time he is uttering it, looks as white as a sheet, and is as monotonous in delivery as possible'. Spooner's account of his preaching bears this out.

> Dr Pusey, [he writes], did not preach often, but when he did preach, preached with a weight and impressiveness which left him without a rival. I still recollect a sermon of his on the guilt of post-Baptismal sin, and the difficulty, if not the impossibility, of repentance for it, based on Hebrews VI. 4–6, which even at this distance of time fills me with apprehension and awe when I think of it. His venerable appearance, bowed as he was then with age and trouble, his subdued, monotonous most solemn voice, his austerity of personal character, witnessed to by manner and gesture alike, a certain aloofness from the world and the things of the world, and absorption in things spiritual and heavenly, gave to what he said an impressiveness and solemnity which it is impossible to describe, but which time does not readily efface.

When Pusey died Spooner noted in his diary

> He is a man who strongly influenced a generation. The great lessons we seem to me to have learnt from him are the continuity of the Church and the continuity of principles which have prevailed in it. He has often mistaken details for principles, but that is an error into which we all fall. In his protest against Calvinism, in his view of religion as a system of training

continued through life I quite agree with him; in the value he attached to the confessional as a moral instrument and as to the desirability of vows I should probably differ from him. Most of all, perhaps, I should object to the raising of the clergy into a separate caste.

Another University preacher whom Spooner describes in the same chapter of his autobiography is H. P. Liddon, Pusey's biographer and one of his most devoted followers. Of him Spooner writes

Very different was Dr Liddon alike in appearance, in temper, in the impression he produced. In authority, impressiveness, spiritual insight and weight, he never attained to the height of Dr Pusey, but to listen to one of his great sermons was a far greater intellectual treat. His clear, thrilling, penetrating voice, the admirable order and lucidity of his discourse, its clear-cut outlines and incisiveness, its picturesque vividness of detail, the exhaustiveness with which the topic was treated, its argumentative power, the flashes of lambent sarcasm with which the argument was lit up, combined to make a perfect whole which it was a delight to listen to, and in fact we flocked in our hundreds to listen to him, and looked forward to the day when we should listen to him again. His well known Bampton Lectures were delivered at this time, and it was these which finally and definitely established his fame as a preacher. Extending, as they many of them did, over more than an hour in length, they carried us on from beginning to end, and our interest never flagged. I well remember how in one at least, coming in late, I had to stand for all of the time; how great a trial it was! and yet how willingly borne rather than forego the treat of listening to it. Yet perhaps as a preacher he suffered from two defects; he was too often combative, when it would have been better for him to be persuasive; and the sarcasm of which he was master, if it wounded, as it often did, was not calculated to win over those whom it wounded.

The then Bishop of Oxford, Samuel Wilberforce, who was Spooner's first cousin once removed, commonly known as 'Soapy Sam', did not impress Spooner, who described him as

rather a disappointment. He was eloquent indeed, and had a beautiful voice, a charming address and extraordinary readiness and adroitness, but he lacked in my judgment, real impressiveness; and though I never for a moment regarded him as insincere, he had not the same note of solemn earnestness and high-souled remoteness as Dr Pusey, nor of passionate intellectual and spiritual conviction as Dr Liddon.

The fourth of these great preachers was William Magee, successively Bishop of Peterborough and Archbishop of York, who was select preacher in the University from 1880 to 1882. Him Spooner describes as

beyond question the finest orator and the most eloquent man I have ever listened to ... I suppose that as is the case with all oratory pure and simple, the effect of his preaching must have been immediately most impressive, but also transitory; for while I can vividly remember the great impression his words had upon me at the time, and the enjoyment it was to listen to him, I cannot now recall the subject of his sermons, nor any of the particular things he said.

In a later chapter he writes of another ecclesiastic, Dean Liddell of Christ Church, perhaps best known to us now as the father of Lewis Carroll's Alice, whom Spooner describes as the most outstanding social figure in Oxford. As an undergraduate, [he goes on] I had no acquaintance with him; he seemed to those of us who were not members of the House, and to some, I fancy, who were, at an almost immeasurable distance from us; but soon after I became a Fellow, I made the acquaintance of him and of Mrs Liddell through my godfather, Archbishop Tait, and received later on not a little kindness and hospitality from them. Dean Liddell was Vice-Chancellor from 1870–74, and was an almost ideal occupant of the Chair. A strong and even ardent Liberal, his tenure of office was marked by an even-handed justice and impartiality which up to that time had certainly not always distinguished the Vice-Chancellors in their bestowal of patronage and in the appointments to Committee and other offices which depended upon them. In the conduct of business again, combining at once despatch with complete freedom of debate, readiness to accept suggestions and patience in listening to them, the Dean is still remembered as an ideal Vice-Chancellor. As a figure-head to the University it would be difficult to surpass him – extremely handsome and dignified, he carried himself as one who, having a high office to fill, wished and intended to fill it worthily. In conversation a certain shyness which he never overcame made him reserved and gave him a certain appearance of hauteur; like Jowett he was unready and even indisposed to begin a conversation, and usually left to his younger inter-locutor the burden of making the first move, some-times a serious one; but his fearlessness and freshness of thought, gave interest to what he said, and the openmindedness and candour with which he could discuss any subject, made him, for those who were brought into intimate relations with him, the most ideal of counsellors and most helpful of friends.

Spooner describes other ecclesiastics in his diary. When Dean Stanley of Westminster, the biographer of Thomas Arnold, died in July 1881, Spooner wrote

His loss is a heavy one. He was the most brilliant talker I have ever met – and I have met Mr Gladstone – so graphic in description, kindling to a story, sharp and pointed. But he was much more than this, a man of a really chivalrous temper, not afraid to stand up for a cause because it was unpopular, straightforward and brave, having the courage of his convictions. He was too very liberal minded and sympathetic and could see good in all kinds of people, churches and agencies. His own faith was, I believe, real though not very definite, in fact he rather disliked a very definite faith, perhaps under-rating the power which it gives,

According to the *D.N.B.* he was reluctant to take orders because of his dislike of the Athanasian Creed.

In his diary Spooner mentions the death of two Archbishops of Canterbury. The first was his uncle by marriage and godfather A. C. Tait, whose Examining Chaplain he had been (see page 104 above). In August 1882 the Archbishop was dying; 'he is very patient and tranquil, equally ready to die or to live, a fitting end to a noble and well-spent life'. In November he died –

The best and kindest man I have known . . . I should like to give some description of him. He was a middle-sized man but gave you the impression of a tall man so dignified was his mien. His face was grave, some people thought stern, but he had a beautiful sweet smile and a twinkle of bright humour in his eye. He was a keen observer of men and a very shrewd judge of character seeing almost always the right man for each particular place. He dearly loved a good story and told them himself remarkably well with a keen

sense of their humour or pathos . . . In public affairs
the qualities which gave him influence were his clear,
calm judgment, his high conception of the part he had
to play and his devotion to it, his great personal
dignity, his sound judgment and fairness and open
mind . . . When near death he said 'If this is dying it is
not so bad' . . . Today (December 10th) Dean Church
sent a stream of cold water down my back by preaching without mention of him on the shortcomings of
religious men – sad that in the grave differences should
not be forgot.

When Tait's successor, Archbishop Benson, died in
October 1896 Spooner was less enthusiastic; 'he was a bit
of an actor but not I think consciously and had a great
delight in stately religious services and ceremonials'. Benson
was succeeded as Archbishop of Canterbury by Frederick
Temple (' "old for the purpose" as was once said of me',
Spooner comments) and of Temple's successor as Bishop of
London, Mandell Creighton, Spooner writes 'he has, I
believe, greatly changed since I knew him; then he was a
moqueur with nothing much but his cleverness and ability
to get on to recommend him; now I believe he is an
earnest man and he certainly wins the confidence both of
clergy and laity which a humbug could hardly do.' This
seems a curiously diminishing comment on the scholarly
author of a history of the Papacy in five volumes.

Spooner rarely comments on public figures. Reading a
life of Gladstone, he comments 'The two features which
impress me most are the high level at which he tried to live
it and largely succeeded and the disturbing force all through
he was in politics'. When Lord Salisbury died in 1903
Spooner wrote 'his was a great figure, aloof and un-
sympathetic, but skilful and disinterested, masterful and

strong'. On Charles Darwin 'the revolution effected by his theory of development is probably overrated at present – certainly the limits of evolution have not yet been accurately determined – yet it has been without doubt an eminently fruitful idea – and has much truth in it, tho' in H. Spencer's hands it has been pushed into many absurdities'.

But of course most of Spooner's characters are of Oxford figures. The most influential of these was Benjamin Jowett. Of him in his early days, before he became Master of Balliol, Spooner has written an interesting first-hand account:

When I began to read for *Literae Humaniores*, Professor Jowett was by far the most influential of my teachers. The question of what salary he ought to receive was then being warmly debated, and I remember attending the delivery of Professor Montague Barnard's judgment on the subject. I cannot but feel that Dr Pusey and those whom he led, made a great mistake in opposing the raising of his stipend. To keep him out of money which he seemed well to have earned, and to which in the judgment of many of us he was justly entitled, did nothing to diminish the influence which he was able to exercise as Professor and secured for him in addition the admiration which even the suspicion of unfair treatment or martyrdom is sure to win. Jowett certainly came to be looked upon as a martyr by us, and we venerated him the more for that. His Lectures on the early Greek Philosophers, and on Plato, which were what we most attended, were not very good. Those on the early Greek Philosophers were not very carefully prepared, nor were they systematic nor thorough. They consisted in great part of translations of passages from Ritter and Preller's handbook, of remarks illustrative of them, and of rather obvious reflexions upon them; so that he was described with some truth by a wit of the time as 'getting up quietly and giving a few faint glimpses into the obvious'. On the other hand, his lectures on Plato contained much shrewd and original criticism of a common sense kind, a good deal of which was embodied in the charming introductions which he wrote to his translation of the Dialogues. The translation of long passages from the Dialogues with which the Lectures were also largely interspersed, were always delightful; and though the manner of delivery was curious, – he used to sing softly to himself, and look out of the window at intervals – it was not ineffectual, and particular sayings of his stuck in the mind and were remembered. But it was in the private interviews, when one took him essays which he received from all members of the University who liked to bring them to him, that one really learnt and gained much. His criticisms, though severe, were just and generally kindly, and he often added to them a word or two of striking force and shrewdness; above all, he never allowed slovenly or confused work to pass uncensured, so that whoever took essays to him, did them with care and thoroughness, and to the best of his ability, and acquired valuable habits thereby. Jowett was a master in the art of developing a capacity for taking pains in his pupils, and such a capacity, though even when raised to its utmost limit it is not genius, is a most serviceable gift to possess. The better he knew you and the more he liked you, the more did he seek to develop this capacity, and in the power which he had in this direction, lay, I believe, the great secret of his influence and success in the case of the very large number of Balliol men whom he started in careers of usefulness and great distinction.

The paper which Spooner wrote and delivered to the New College Essay Society after his retirement, entitled *Two*

Oxford Reformers, Mark Pattison and Benjamin Jowett (see page 60) gives a much less vivid picture. In July 1891 Spooner wrote in his diary 'I dined . . . with Strachan Davidson at Balliol . . . I sat by Jowett and we talked much about old pupils. I asked him whom he considered the ablest of all his pupils; he answered Asquith'. When Jowett died on 1 October 1893 Spooner wrote 'he will be greatly missed in Oxford, a real force gone out of the place. In University matters he had become in later life a steadying and even a conservative force'.

Spooner also characterises at some length the leading figures at the University Museum, which in those days constituted the Science Area of the University. The most important of these was Sir Henry Acland, the Professor of Medicine, who, as Spooner writes,

> having successfully carried the erection of the Museum in the two previous decades, was watching over its organisation, and gathering around him a band of disciples fitted to carry on and extend the teaching of Science at Oxford, of which he had himself done so much to lay the foundations. Dr Acland was at this time in the prime of his life and activity, and possessed an influence in Oxford which admitted excellence in his profession, the steady and successful pursuit of an ideal consistently followed during many years, great kindness and high character, could not but command. If the University sometimes laughed at him for a certain naive conceit which he occasionally exhibited, they laughed at him with affection and not with bitterness, and felt that it was an amiable foible in a character at once simple and high-souled. While there had already begun to declare itself a certain divergence in aim as to the direction which medical studies should take in Oxford and as to the ground which they should

cover, which grew more pronounced in later years, young and old alike, who were attached to the Museum, recognised him as their leader, a leader without whose insight, courage and pertinacity, science would not have attained in Oxford the position which it had already reached. If the Museum did not satisfy the artistic taste of all of us, over whom the Gothic revival did not exercise the fascination which it had had for a previous generation; and if some of us felt that it had been too ambitious in its design, and that better results might have been obtained had it been allowed to grow up more gradually, so that its constituent parts might have been more fully adapted to the needs of the different branches of science, as they successively disclosed themselves, – against this we recognised that the building as planned was the embodiment of a great idea – the unity and correlation of the different branches of natural knowledge, and we were thankful to Dr Acland for the emphatic expression which in the Museum he had given to this far-reaching conception. Some years later, when the question of a site for the erection of the new Examination Schools was before the University, Dr Acland pleaded with fervour and eloquence for placing them on the site of the existing Botanical Gardens, and for moving the Gardens themselves up into the Parks in the neighbourhood of the Museum, since this would be a further step taken in the direction of unifying the study of the different branches of Natural knowledge. His plea did not prevail, for reasons partly sentimental, partly practical, admirably set forth in a convincing speech by Professor Ingram Bywater; but experience has since convinced many of us that, while the site in the High Street, the Angel site, as it was called from the Old Inn which had previously occupied it, was probably the best which could have been chosen for the new Schools, and is indeed admirably adapted for its purpose, there was more to be said for moving the Botanical Gardens to the neighbourhood of the Museum than at the time we recognised, and that not inconsiderable inconveniences have been caused in the teaching of certain branches of science by the local separation of the Botanical Gardens and the Botanical Lecture Rooms from the home of the cognate branches of science with which the study of Botany is, and must always remain, closely associated. So far the contention of Dr Acland has been completely vindicated.

It would be impossible to leave these reminiscences of Dr Acland and of the position which in the seventies he occupied in Oxford, without saying a word about Mrs Acland and their house in Broad Street. As an undergraduate I had no acquaintance with them, but circumstances caused me to know them not intimately but fairly well, soon after I became a Fellow. Their home seemed to me from the first, in many ways an ideal one characterised by great family affection, by a freedom from state and ceremony but a genuine spirit of hospitality and a wonderful charity, good-will and sympathy for all those with whom they were brought into contact. An evening party at their house was a real pleasure, unconventional but full of good company, good talk, good music, good spirits and happiness. Dr Acland was, I will not say at his best on these occasions, but certainly the life and soul of the party. Of Mrs Acland I stood slightly in awe, for I found her just a little prim, perhaps a little masterful; but of her deep religious feeling and true kindness of heart there could be no doubt, nor of the skill with which she managed her delightful, but somewhat wayward, husband and the different members of the family whose guide and wise counsellor she was. Of the hold she had in Oxford and of the high esteem in which she was held, ample proof was furnished by the

unanimity with which the Home and the Association
for District Nurses connected with it, which were
erected in her memory, were supported by all classes
of the community.

After a brief reference to J. Phillips, the Professor of
Geology and first Keeper of the Museum, Spooner turns to
George Rolleston, the Professor of Anatomy and Physio-
logy, whom he recalls as

the greatest combination of intellectual and moral
force that I have ever come across. Every word and
almost every gesture was full of energy. A fearless
lover of truth and seeking it in every direction, it was
to the study of man in every aspect, whether as a
physical, and intellectual, or a moral and spiritual
being, that all the force of his powers was directed.
While siding unhesitatingly with Huxley in his con-
troversy with Professor Owen and the Bishop of
Oxford, as to the similarity or even identity of man on
the physical side with the anthropoid apes, Rolleston
yet refused to admit that this derogated in any way
from the dignity of man in his higher developments,
or assimilated him in his spiritual nature to the apes
from which, perhaps, he was sprung. The lower stages
do not, he maintained, preclude, they only furnish the
basis for, the higher; and the best way to realise what
man can be, is to study what he has been and the
various stages by which he has reached the position
which he now occupies. But while building on this
foundation he never for a moment doubted the
importance and value of man's moral and spiritual
aspirations and convictions, however he may have
come by them. They were facts to be taken into
account and held by, as much as the facts of the external world, and man's physical frame, and to ignore
them or make light of them would simply be to dis-

regard the requirements of truth. In this way he combined an unalterable loyalty to the cause of what he recognised as truth with a loyalty equally unalterable to man's moral and spiritual inheritance, and to all that that inheritance implied.

When Rolleston died in 1881, Spooner wrote in his diary that

I consider [him] as one of the most remarkable men I have met. Mrs Grote once described him as that intellectual steam engine and that was the exact impression he gave, an impression of always working, speaking, thinking at high pressure. In speaking he always emphasised every word, most of all the little ones. I fancy he did much the same in thinking. He was a man of a great variety of interests and animated with a genuine desire to get at the truth in each one of them. But to me the greatest interest of him was that he was a man passionately scientific but also most truly religious and interested as well in Theology. He helped to bridge over one of the chasms which divide Oxford; each year there seem fewer bridges left. There is no one marked out to succeed him . . . Lankaster*, who is perhaps intellectually fitted, would be a moral misfortune to the place, being bitterly anti-Christian and not, so far as I know, a man of high character.

Another Oxford character whom Spooner describes at length in his autobiography is the philosopher, T. H. Green. Of him Spooner writes

The years from 1870–1880 mark the rise and culmination of the philosophical influence of T. H. Green. His influence told in two different directions. On the

*Sic. Probably he means Professor Sir Ray Lankester (1847–1929), who did in fact succeed Rolleston.

one hand his actual system was hard and abstract, a sort of aftermath of Hegelianism; yet partly because it was a reaction against the exaggerated individualism of Mill and Spencer, partly because it was intended as a vindication and defence of fundamental moral and spiritual truths, above all, because Green himself was a strong personality and represented a powerful moral force, his teaching exercised a strong fascination over the minds of successive generations of undergraduates who came to be taught by him. Men felt confirmed and strengthened in their religious beliefs and in their moral aspirations, when at the back of those beliefs and those aspirations they had such an intellectual force as Green wielded. With the particular form their beliefs and aspirations assumed, he might not sympathise, and yet on the main issue he was at one with them; in support of beliefs and hopes of that kind he could bring arguments to bear, and he could suggest arguments that they might bring in defence of them – arguments, which, however little they might be appreciated by the general public, were the sort of arguments which alone made a consistent system of philosophy, or a coherent account of knowledge, possible. In this way, while Green himself was on the side of Liberalism, and had, I think, little sympathy with the Church party as such, rather favouring a Christianity which verged upon Unitarianism and was expressed in the somewhat indefinite formulae of undenominationalism, yet the Church party drew many arguments in support of their cause from his armoury, and approached their subject from points of view which his philosophy suggested. No one, for instance, can read 'Lux Mundi' and not feel how much the writers of several of the articles in it have been influenced alike in the results that they have obtained, and still more, perhaps, in their mode of stating them, by the teaching of Green.

When he died in 1882, Spooner wrote in his diary

He will be missed both in the city and in the University. In the University his influence, particularly among the clever men, was very great: most of them who attended his lectures, embraced or were greatly influenced by his system of philosophy. His philosophy was Hegelian in the main but with a good deal of his own in it. He was very anti-materialist, but leaned I suppose in religion to a kind of pantheism. As far as I could follow him, I agreed in much that he said as to the extent to which our own conditions of thought must enter into the construction of knowledge, but there was a certain element in which I could never follow him, an element in which he seemed to say that the mind created its own sensations as well as gave form and coherence to them. He influenced greatly many of those who differed much from him in his conclusions . . . His philosophy teaching was no doubt the central factor in philosophy at Oxford. In Politics he was a very staunch Liberal and supporter of Mr Gladstone. He had a great hatred of corruption and insisted on the election enquiry here. He was not a good talker and in later years suffered much from heart disease, which discoloured his face.

Spooner in his diary does not allude to the perhaps best-known philosopher ever to be attached to New College, John Cook Wilson, who as Wykeham Professor of Logic was a Fellow of the College from 1889 until his death in 1915. But in a letter to Rashdall dated October 9th 1903 he writes 'Between ourselves cannot you induce Cook Wilson to write something connected instead of frittering away his energy on small points which do not matter? I have tried but to no avail'.

Much later, Spooner wrote in his diary about another well-known Oxford philosopher. In 1923 he recorded that

> F. H. Bradley, Senior Fellow of Merton, died suddenly and unexpectedly this week and was buried on Tuesday the 23rd [September]. He was a Philosopher, the greatest of modern English Philosophers and was given the O.M. for his excellence in Philosophy. Joachim our Professor of Logic and at this time Subwarden of the College was a great friend and follower of Bradley and I tried to make out from him in what the excellence of Bradley's philosophy consisted, but I failed. Bradley's book on Appearance and Reality laid no hold on my mind at all. It seems to me a destruction of all appearance and a search into absolute reality which can never be caught, because we have no power with which to apprehend it, and the contradictions between those who profess to apprehend it are so great that I cannot believe that any of them has reached the absolute truth or is endowed with the faculty for reaching it.

Some other Oxford characters of less significance are described at length. Others again, about whom we might have welcomed more information, are dismissed summarily. When Pater died, all Spooner could find to say in his diary was 'He seems to have changed much as the years went on and Bassett wrote an account of him which took the world by surprise. He had been judged hardly: and the mistakes made about him should be a warning against harsh judgments'. When Professor Freeman, the eminent historian, Froude's great enemy, died in Spain in 1892, Spooner comments, a little obscurely, that

> though he quarrels a good deal with things as they are, he still brings a breath of outside criticism to bear upon

them and so helps to keep them fresh and sweet. As a writer I have never been able to give him a very high place; I think him wanting in the sense of perspective and proportion, and to be a man of few ideas, but he was a genuine lover of truth, and took much pains to ascertain it, though his prejudices, I think, often made him fail to reach it.

Spooner's characters are of intrinsic interest for the personalities, not all faded, whom he describes. They also shed some light on Spooner himself. We see the characteristics he values, integrity, good nature, the search for truth, religious faith. We see too that though he is generally benevolent he can be quite sharp when he feels sharpness is in place; this too was a marked feature of his own character in other fields. In characterising himself he has left these features out, but from his writings and from others' descriptions of him, one can see that he in fact possessed them.

CHAPTER VIII

Spooner's Travels

SPOONER TRAVELLED MAINLY in England. His diary is full of accounts of journeyings to and fro across the island, of all-day walks in the Pennines, in Cornwall and in the Lake District. On one occasion, staying at Grasmere in August 1893, he pays an interesting call: 'We rowed across the lake to Brantwood and had lunch there and saw all Ruskin's treasures, including the six priceless Turners, the sole ornament of his plain little bedroom, and Ruskin himself. Ruskin was still very poorly but talked a little about his own writings'. At some point after he became Warden he and his wife acquired a house, How Foot, in the Lakes, and spent much of their vacation time there.

But he did go abroad occasionally. I have mentioned (see footnote on p. 130) the mystery about his visit to America. In 1890 he went to the Tyrol: 'Of our travels there', he writes in his diary, 'I have written an account in another book', but this has disappeared. In September 1903, during his first Long Vacation as Warden, he went to Dresden.

The early days of our stay there, [he wrote in his diary after he got back] were exceedingly hot and of them we spent a good deal on the river, while Frank had often to rest in her room. It afterwards turned stormy and wet and then cold and dark . . . We spent a good deal of our time in the Gallery, more than half the mornings we were in Dresden . . . ['I doubt if I know a good picture from a bad one' Spooner had written after a visit to the Royal Academy in 1881, but this did not restrain him from 'lionising', to use his peculiar expression, the sights of Dresden] . . . and it grew upon us all the time we were there. Not only is the San Sisto the Prince of pictures but the Rembrandts, Paul Veronese, Tintarello [sic] and the Dutch and Flemish School are also splendid. Cath would add the Rubens also, but they do not appeal to me so much . . . Besides the Gallery we saw the Green Vaults, that curious collection in which the Kings of Saxony have got together the greatest accumulation of portable valuables in the world; the sculpture gallery; the museum of antiquities and the splendid China collections.

When they visited the Meissen porcelain factory he noticed that 'much freedom is allowed to the artists, who have a sort of copy for the main idea, but are allowed to treat the details as they like. Unluckily they cannot escape, any more than we do, the horrors of lead glazes'. The Spooners also went to the opera –

The Flying Dutchman, the music of which I always like, though it grows tedious towards the end; after that *Tannhäuser*, which I understood and followed better than I had before; I place it second among Wagner's operas, the *Meister-Singer* [sic] first. The last week we heard three parts of *The Ring*. I care for these less than Wagner's other operas. They seem to me wearisome and fine only in parts . . . the opening scene of *The Rheingold* is pretty and the final scene impressive; between there is a wilderness: *The Valkyrie* is fine almost throughout and Wotan is not in it the bore he is in the other two . . . The orchestra is often

fine and impressive, but when one's thoughts are
diverted by the acting, it is hard for an unmusical
person like myself to follow it. On the whole I am
glad to have heard it but my view that the Opera is
artistically a mistake is in no ways shaken.

In a letter to Rashdall on his return he wrote 'I have learnt
some little German while I was at Dresden and know more
than I ever did before, but it is not much'.

In the spring of 1912 he made his longest journey. For
the first time for fifty years he missed a term at Oxford. He
had been advised to rest, and set off with two of his
daughters on a sea voyage to South Africa. The voyage is
described in a series of letters to Mrs Spooner, which
Spooner had typed out on his return. They took a small
ship, with a captain whom Spooner describes as 'a roughish
seaman'. Spooner was clearly a good sailor, and was soon
pestering the captain to let him hold services, even in rough
weather in the Bay of Biscay. But this proved impossible;
'we had quite a troubled night and shipped some water, and
I have never been knocked about so much in my berth'.
Later 'the sea got up in the night, and just after our early
service while we were waiting for breakfast, a huge wave
landed on deck, poured down the companion ladder, and
flooded most of our cabins; it spoilt my books and my
writing paper but did little other mischief, nor did the girls
into whose cabin it also came, suffer much harm'. They
touched at Las Palmas, and passed 'Cape de Verde, the
extreme west point of Africa . . . On the long reef of rocks
which runs out almost from the Cape itself lay a German
steamer wrecked, to remind one of the possible dangers of
the sea'. They called at Ascension, 'a curious volcanic coal
heap, quite bare of vegetation', and at St Helena, 'extra-

ordinarily rocky and barren but with a fine outline and some trees and green in the interior – a fitting place for a prison and not much else'. While there 'we were much shocked to hear of the loss of the *Titanic* which of course comes home to us painfully. These vast ships seem to be on too vast a scale to be manageable or safe. Two thousand people cannot be provided for or controlled in an emergency'. As they approached Capetown 'Rosemary was allowed to try her hand at steering the ship, but did not make much of it, as she would have steered us dead on to the barren coast of Africa. I felt safer in the hands of the Steersman'.

They arrived in Capetown at the end of April. Their life there seems to have been social and agreeable, without political or racial overtones. 'I met Botha and had a little talk with him', Spooner writes, 'and he has asked me to lunch with him one day – but I am doubtful if I can'. Later he lunched at Government House; 'His Excellency* was very gracious, and Cath had a long talk with him at lunch, and after lunch he poured out his whole soul to me for an hour. He has grown rather stout, and feels cooped up here among the English who are all ultra Conservative, while he remains an impenitent but not very powerful Liberal'. Then they visited Blomfontein (where the Administrator was 'in bad odour as he favours the Dutch') and Kimberley ('a very quiet little place, very simple and not at all smart') where the Bishop 'absorbingly High Church, can see no merit in anything but the Cathedral and its services, and regards the Dutch who are very Protestant, simply as aliens and enemies'. Spooner always disliked intolerance. Next they went to the Victoria Falls ('surpassingly beautiful'), to

*This was Viscount Gladstone, youngest son of the Prime Minister.

Rhodes's grave in the Matopo Hills and back to Bulawayo and Johannesburg. Everywhere he went he seems to have met New College men, or if they failed there was always a Bishop to entertain him and give him a pulpit in his Cathedral. After a stay on an up-country farm the Spooners returned to Capetown, and early in July set sail for England, this time in a more comfortable ship, the *Grantully Castle*; one of the passengers was 'Mr Reitz, the old man who gave us such trouble in the War by stirring up all the governments of Europe against us. He has a charming daughter, also a great little rebel, who is very enthusiastic and very well educated, and talks literature and other things to me'. They got back on 24 July and next day 'except that I am feeling very well and strong and vigorous, I am as if I had never been away . . . our voyage was just a treat from beginning to end, calm and fine and cool all the way'. The voyage he refers to was the voyage home, but the adjectives he uses would do for the whole trip. He was clearly quite unaware of the slow-burning volcano on which the British-controlled administration in South Africa was sitting. Spooner was not a political animal.

CHAPTER IX

The End

IN 1924, after an interval of seventeen years, Spooner began to write in his diary again. His handwriting has become shaky, and he is even vaguer than usual about dates, not surprisingly perhaps since he was now eighty. He begins 'I wrote in this Book under date of March 1903 an account of my entry on the Wardenship and of a few of the impressions which I then received'. One might expect him to go on to announce that he now intends to describe the conclusion of his Wardenship, but instead he continues 'We came back from a visit to William and Mardie at Ilkley on Wednesday September 17 and began on College business at once. The remainder of the week was largely taken up with interviews, committees and College business'. Then comes the reference to Bradley's death quoted in Chapter VII and he continues with a rather humdrum account of his daily doings. Only gradually does it emerge that we are leading up to his resignation at the end of December 1924. He presided at his last Stated General Meeting of the College in October, and at the Gaude, which in those years was held in that month, he made two speeches; in one of them 'a speech which pleased them', the main point was 'the remark of a lady who said early in my Wardenship that it would be "nice" if there were 40 Wardens instead of 39; while I neither then nor even now, thought it would be nice tho' it might be necessary'. Presumably this was the speech which contained the veiled allusion to spoonerisms (see page 137). Next Sunday, the first in Full Term, 'I preached in Chapel, and tried to enforce upon the men the responsibility involved in an University life and their time at Oxford'. Throughout the term the Spooners were entertaining briskly, among others Herbert Baker,

> the Architect who has just completed the new War Memorial at Winchester. He has come to Oxford to see about a new Building for the Rhodes Trustees which they are proposing to build on a site at the end of Wadham's Garden for a great sum . . . Baker is a very nice fellow, a South African with a special gift for making his buildings suit their surroundings. He has built buildings for the South African administration at Pretoria and is along with Lutyens building the new Government Buildings at Delhi. We had young Herzog, son of the Nationalist Prime Minister in South Africa to meet them.

At the end of term a spate of farewell parties broke out. At one of these Professor Manning remembers Spooner saying

> For more than three-quarters of my life I have been at New College. For the first quarter of my life I was too *young* to be a member of the College. For the last quarter of my life I have been too *old* to be anything else but Warden. But for the remaining half of my life I think I may claim that I did what lay in my power to serve the College. And in that I found my happiness and my *great reward*.

Many letters were written to him at the time of his retirement. Spencer Leeson, for instance, the future Headmaster of Winchester and Bishop of Peterborough, then just beginning to teach at Winchester, wrote that

You will know, without any need for me to say it, what your old pupils and friends are thinking as the time for your retirement approaches; and I wish you could hear the affectionate things that are being said of you here. Whoever your successor may be, to us who were at the College under you, you will always be the Warden of New College . . . and if the hundreds of students who have passed through your hands have as much to thank you for as I have, then the body of affection and gratitude that you will be carrying with you into your retirement will indeed be great . . . You seem to sum up in yourself the history of the College since its great days began, and how much you have contributed to the history and the greatness.

Ernest Barker wrote 'Jowett, I daresay, will long be remembered. But would it have been such happiness to work in Balliol under Jowett as it was to work in New College when you were Warden? You may say that happiness is not the criteria of your success. But the Head of a College who can make its teachers happy in their work has done a great thing for his College'. Randall Davidson, then Archbishop of Canterbury and Spooner's cousin by marriage, wrote that during Spooner's sixty-two years at New College he had been

continuously filling an active and vigorous part in College life, and latterly have been both captain and pilot for the ship in waters which were not always smooth; while at the same time the College has been advancing both numerically and in all sorts of other ways, and now instead of laying down the position because of failing powers you are by common consent as vigorous to all appearance as you were twenty years ago! I have heard of your speeches this year and of your administrative work, and in all manner of ways you are, to the best of my belief, abreast of whatever is strong and dominant in the Oxford life of to-day. I have always looked to you as wielding a steadying influence in Oxford life and as among the sanest of its chief men.

On Archbishop Davidson and others Spooner at this time evidently made an impression of serene strength and self-confidence. But his diary tells a different story.

This saying good-bye, [Spooner wrote] has left me with a very blank feeling as if the object of my life had gone, and I had nothing left but to prepare myself for death, and for that I am ill equipped. This feeling has grown upon me since and I still feel the preparation a hard matter and haunting doubts come upon me. 'Lord increase my faith' has to be now my constant prayer.

At the annual dinner given for the College tenants he was 'sick and ill and with difficulty got through my speech so at the rent dinner I was able to say but little and it passed off rather flatly; but I shook hands with the Tenants and they seemed sorry to part'. Finally,

on the 31st my Wardenship came to an end. I lay it down with great regret and deliver up my house to the College with regret also. The Fellows think I have been a good Warden and have all contributed to give me a personal present, while the ladies have given Frank one too. On the whole the College has prospered under me and the Fellows have been happy and friendly among themselves and I have enjoyed my

beautiful house and high estate. I have won the praise
of men but not the praise of God. God keep thou me
from my secret faults which are many and great and
have led me into that scepticism and want of faith in
which I so often wallow, which spoils my prayers and
mars my efforts after holiness and my desire to do
good. Lord increase my faith.

This is sad enough, but there is worse to come. Under a
heading 'January 1 1925' the diary continues

I began the new year, no longer Warden of New
College, with a very dull and deadened feeling, rather
lost not knowing what to turn myself to, or what to
do; nor have I wholly lost this sense even now when I
am writing this three months later. At first I was rather
buoyed up by hoping that I might bring out a new
edition of my *Histories of Tacitus*, but Messrs. Mac-
millan, who had originally published the Book and
the University Press to whom I also offered it both
declined it. This was a disappointment to me, as when
first published it had received a good deal of praise
from the critics and had helped to gain me admission
to the Athenaeum Club; but I was conscious in my
heart that it was not a very thorough bit of work and
so I acquiesced, tho' I was rather at a loss what other
piece of work to turn to.

Then came the question of his successor. There were two
candidates, H. A. L. Fisher and P. E. Matheson, the latter a
College tutor and ancient historian who wrote the account
of Spooner that appears in the *D.N.B.*

The 14 of January, [Spooner writes in his diary,] was
the day of the College meeting almost the first at
which for twenty years I have not presided and I felt
the shock of being left out in the cold. The fellows had
had a preliminary meeting some days before at which

they had determined to pass over Matheson and take
Fisher.* I should have preferred Matheson as being the
more religious man and more likely to keep up the
traditions of the place familiar to me, but Fisher was
undoubtedly the more distinguished and the more of
a figure-head. I think that Mrs Fisher will have more
difficulty in getting on with the fellows and the undergraduates than Mrs Matheson would have had; but I
think either would have made quite good and sufficient
heads. We shall go away regretted, for we have been
hospitable, have become from our long residence
something of an institution and I have a certain gift of
making friends with the men convincing them that I
really thought of them and cared for their interests. I
had many letters attesting this; by the Fellows my wife
was valued for her courtesy and hospitality, and I
because I took a wide view of my office and cared for
every side of College life, the Fellows, the undergraduates, the incumbents, the tenants and the servants.

After a brief reference to the installation of his successor
the diary peters out: 'On Monday February 1 I left Oxford
being taken up to London by Sir H. Allen in the early
morning in his motor car and landed safely at Catherine's
at 22 Montague Square by 10 a.m. In the afternoon I called
on Mrs Wickham and Toby Moon'. After that there are no
more entries, except for some unexplained extracts from
sermons.

The Spooners moved to No. 1 Canterbury Road, a
large, typically North Oxford house on a corner site by the

---

*Fisher was at this time a back-bench M.P., out of office since the fall of
Lloyd George but very reluctant to leave politics. When someone asked him
if it was true he was thinking of becoming Warden of New College he
replied 'It may come to that'. This remark was reported back to the Fellows
and nearly lost him the election.

Banbury Road (now the House of St Gregory and St
Macrina, the centre of Oxford's Orthodox Church community). They lived there in some style and comfort, and
no one who encountered them would have sensed the
feelings of despairing unhappiness which pervade the last
entries in Spooner's diary. He seemed tranquil and serene;
perhaps the immediate impact of his retirement, after a continuous membership of New College of sixty-two years,
induced a melancholy which proved transitory. He was in
constant communication with the old members; typical
was a letter he received in September 1927 from Sir Esme
Howard, then British Ambassador in Washington, about
one of his sons who had died while at New College. The
boy had written out some prayers which his father had had
privately printed, and in sending a copy to Spooner Sir
Esme wrote 'He always spoke of you with such affection
that I count you as one of his principal friends, and therefore hasten to send you a copy'.

The Spooners continued to entertain New College
undergraduates, particularly if they were Scholars or sons
of one of his old pupils (I was both). One of Spooner's last
acts as Warden had been to preside over the election of five
Winchester Scholars – 'fair average Scholars but I do not
think more' he wrote in his diary. Two of these Scholars
were John Sparrow and myself. After Spooner's retirement
we were in due course invited to Canterbury Road;
describing his visit, John Sparrow has written

> My memory of the occasion is not at all points distinct
> from that of many another North Oxford tea-party;
> but I recall the kindly welcome given the guests by the
> Misses Spooner and, seated a little apart after tea was
> over, the diminutive pink and white figure of Warden

Spooner himself. One by one we were taken up to him for a little conversation. When my turn came he put to me a few conventional questions – what School was I reading? Had I pleasant rooms? What was the general nature of my interests? – and when these were duly answered he went on to say: 'I hope you will have a happy time at Oxford. I am sure you will. But, if you will take the advice of an old man' – I am a little doubtful about that introductory sentence, not at all about the words that followed – '*beware of the lure of men and women*'. This surprising injunction, quickly and quietly uttered, impressed itself indelibly upon my mind, and though I have never been sure what exactly was the warning it was intended to convey, I have always done my best to follow the general line it seemed to indicate.

New College undergraduates were not the Spooners' only guests. On one occasion Professor Oscar Veblen of Princeton, a nephew of the more famous Thorstein Veblen, was spending a term as a visiting professor at New College, and he and Mrs Veblen were invited to tea in Canterbury Road. When the day came Mrs Veblen had a cold and sent a message excusing herself. When Veblen arrived he was greeted by the ex-Warden, with Mrs Spooner standing massively beside him. 'How do you do?' said Spooner. 'I'm so sorry – you won't – have the pleasure – of – meeting my wife'.

Spooner used not infrequently to come into New College to dine after his retirement. On one occasion, being asked how he was, he replied 'I'm very well, thank you – *brutally* well'. A pause. 'But – I'm not as – *clever* – as I used to be'.* Professor Manning has described what seems to have been his last visit to the College;

*I owe this anecdote and the Veblen story to Sir Christopher Cox.

There were few of us there. Towards the hour, I think 9.30, when he was to be collected at the Lodge and taken home, several of us escorted him to the gate. Emerging from Upper Senior Common Room and having been helped on with his overcoat, Spooner, flanked by taller friends, stood looking up at the long familiar line of pegs. 'I must now' he said slowly, 'Annex the best cap I can find'. Those were the last words I can remember hearing him utter.

The Spooners celebrated their golden wedding in the summer of 1928. On August 29th 1930, after an illness of several months, Spooner died peacefully. He was buried at Grasmere, near his home at How Foot. In his life of Bishop Butler Spooner wrote of the Bishop

He is always personal. A writer so transparently single-hearted and so scrupulously honest as Butler was, can scarcely fail to be this. He lets you see, and cannot help doing so, what are his deepest convictions, his strongest motives, his most enduring affections, his keenest interests; in a less degree what are his prevailing dislikes and repulsions. He is on such points absolutely frank with his reader and feels the strongest obligation to be nothing less. He never plays with his subject, never disguises, never holds back, never writes for effect. All is the sincere outcome of an honest and scrupulous mind, set out with all possible care, circumspection and self-restraint. The style, the laboured but carefully chosen words, the cumbrous sentences, adequately and faithfully reflect the inward thought; and so, as we read the writings, we feel with absolute conviction that we know the man.

Spooner would never have claimed for himself that he possessed Butler's intellectual distinction and power. Nevertheless as we read these words we cannot help feeling that Spooner is, quite unconsciously, portraying himself.

Bibliography

Barker, Sir Ernest, *Age and Youth*

Bowra, Sir Maurice, *Memories*

Cooper, A. Duff, *Old Men Forget*

Horton, R. F., *Autobiography*

Laver, James, *Museum Pieces*

Matthews, T. S., *Name and Address*

Oman, Sir C., *Memories of Victorian Oxford*

Rashdall and Rait, *History of New College*

Smith, A. H., *New College Oxford and Its Buildings*

Spooner, W. A., *The Histories of Tacitus*

Spooner, W. A., *Bishop Butler*

Toynbee, A. J., *Acquaintances*

Ward, Mrs Humphrey, *A Writer's Recollections*

Waterfield, Gordon, *Professional Diplomat*

Woolley, Sir Leonard, *Dead Towns and Living Men*

Index